The Holy Mother Mary is God

Dedicated Lightworker Press

KEVIN PETER KELLY
WITH
MARINA NIKOLE KELLY

Published by Spirit Rock INC. DBA Dedicated Lightworker Press
www.Dedicatedlightworker.com ❁ Distributed in the United States
by Pathway Book Service Phone: 1-800-345-6665 www.pathwaybook.com

Editorial Supervision: Caroline Oceana Ryan ❁ Cover Design: Todor Vasilev
Interior Design: Mushtaq Najmi ❁ Format Design: Elaine Brown
Glossary Creation: Lesley Singleton and Kevin Peter Kelly

Library of Congress Cataloging-in Publication Data
Kelly, Kevin Peter 1959-
The Holy Mother Mary is GOD/Kevin Peter Kelly. -1st ed.
1) Spirituality 2) Jesus 3) Religion

Library of Congress Control Number: 2013950349

Tradepaper ISBN: 978-1-62954-000-9
Hardcover ISBN: 978-1-62954-001-6
Digital ISBN: 978-1-62954-002-3

14 13 12 11 10 / 10 9 8 7 6 5 4 3 2 1
1st edition 2013

Printed in the United States of America

Acknowledgements

I give my ultimate gratitude to these
Beautiful Divine Beings of Source and of God,
for they have written most of this book:

The Holy Mother, the Holy Spirit
Saint Joseph (Saint Germain)
Jesus
Malachi
The Great White Brotherhood of Light

I most graciously thank my wife Marina, for she is the heart,
the love and the balance of my life.

I thank my son, Vaju. Through him and Marina
I have found the Oneness that close intimate relationships can give.
He is the son and the Sun of our life.

I thank the one we call the Oracle, who has been with
Malachi for more than thirty-five years.
She has graciously made this work possible.
She truly embodies the Spirit of this book, the Holy Spirit.

I thank the Holy Spirit. She has been with us from the beginning.
She has been my guide my entire life.
The more I love Her, the more I know myself.

I thank Jesus,
for He brought me into Himself and Himself into me.
He is truly the Prince of Peace
and the Son of God.

I thank Saint Joseph,
for He has been with me my entire life.
He is always there to help me like a Father,
the Holy Father that He truly is.

I thank Malachi,
for he has blessed us with his Love and wisdom
and he has taught us Grace by being it.

This is a writing that contains the purity of truth about
God
The Holy Spirit
The Divine Mother
The Holy Mother
The Holy Human
and
The Holy Trinity

Table of Contents

Introduction

Meeting the Holy Trinity

These are the words of our blessed Mother Mary, as received by Marina Nikole Kelly:

Meet the Holy Mother

Dear Children, greetings to you. I am Mother Mary. As you are reading this book, you are going through some questions and doubts. Yes, this book has a lot to be questioned, [but] only if you are using only your mind [while] reading it.

I highly encourage you to read this book using your heart. Let your heart do its discernment, let your heart decide whether this is what you are looking for, or it is not.

My beautiful children, everything you come in contact with is the Divine, a beautiful purity of the Divine Energy. I would like you to treat this book as a great part of the Divine, radiating its true essence to your body, your cellular system. This book can help you to find the truth you are looking for, and [that] was hidden from you for a very long time.

Let this book inspire you, and help you to learn who

you truly are and why you are all here, how beautiful it is to live your life here, and how beautiful you all are.

This is truly a blessing. Enjoy this book and share it with others, as they will benefit from reading it.

I am sending you My blessings of Love and Peace. I am Mother Mary.

Meet the Son

A message received by Marina Nikole Kelly, from Jesus:

Your husband is writing a beautiful book of Mary. We are celebrating his every effort [that] he takes to make it happen. Thank you to both of you. Thank you!

Jesus, who was called Yeshua during His most famous Earth life, gave us the following message for everyone:

Dear Ones, greetings. I am Jesus, [also called] Joshua. I am here to speak my words to you. You are reading this book to find the information you were looking for. You are reading it for a reason.

Let your body absorb the information first. Do not decide so fast whether it is what you were looking for or it is not. Let your body absorb what you are reading, what you are experiencing. You might experience some great bodily changes. All are coming from reading this book.

This book is charged with a high vibrational energy,

and carries a lot of Light. You might start experiencing what we call Light frequencies passing through your body. So when it happens, a lot of people will start to experience body aches, overall tiredness and willingness to go sleep and rest. Celebrate those symptoms, as you are being rewired to match the higher vibrational energies of this book.

You might fall asleep as soon as you start reading this book; allow it to happen. This is the energy of Light coming from this book, to help you not only to read this book and absorb its words and sentences, but to also absorb the great Light of the Divine that this book is charged with.

Enjoy your reading, and be in Peace. I am Jesus, your beloved Brother, sending you my great Love and appreciation. Thank you!

Meet the Holy Father

The next message is from Saint Germain, also known as Saint Joseph, Jesus' Earthly Father.

Greetings, dear ones. I am Saint Germain [Saint Joseph]. As you are reading this book, feel the energies of each word that you are reading. Absorb what is being told to you.

This book is quite unique, and carries the higher intention of the authors to bring Peace and Love on Earth. Appreciate his and her effort to help you and to heal you. You are all the Children of the Divine, living together in this great world.

These words were spoken by Mother Mary, Jesus

and Saint Joseph, who also incarnated as Saint Germain. Thousands of people around the world are now speaking to Divine beings and Angels, and my wife Marina and I are among them.

I have found that people seem to know either a great deal about this phenomenon or almost nothing at all about it. If you are among the latter group, we welcome you, and hope that you will take in these messages with an open heart.

I have been studying the miracle of channeled messages from the Company of Heaven for more than thirty years. I have spoken to Angels and other beings from the Other Side for quite some time, though I'd never found what I would call a clear and direct connection to the Angels until I met the woman we call the Oracle. She has been speaking to Angels for more than sixty years, and to our beloved Malachi for more than thirty-five years. She is the channel by which most of the information in this book came to us.

My wife Marina and I were introduced to the Oracle by a very spiritually gifted friend in 2011. We then began having sessions in which we received the words of Malachi, best known from his Earth life as the great Hebrew prophet of the same name. We have been receiving his messages, channeled through the Oracle, about once a month.

After a few months of these sessions, we came to the realization that when we were speaking with Malachi, we were also speaking to a group consciousness known as the Great White Brotherhood of Light. This group, referred to throughout this book as simply the Great White Brotherhood, is the group consciousness of Mother/Father God, Jesus, the Archangels, and all of the Divine beings who have graced the Earth with their human incarnations. They are the ones who have mastered this realm of matter we call Earth. They are also referred to as the Ascended Masters. We have learned that many Ascended Masters are also Archangels.

The Brotherhood consists of higher beings of Light and energy who have incarnated into many different races and cultures throughout history. "Brotherhood" is a general term, as they have lived Earth lives as both men and women. Each embodies both masculine and feminine traits. The term "White" does not refer to race, but simply to the white Light that permeates and surrounds them.

As Mother Mary said at the start, please read this book with your heart. When entering here, leave your old beliefs and preconceptions at the door. You may pick some of them back up as you are reading. Others will remain left behind for good. In their place will be a new message of Divine Love and Light, which you need no Earthly set of rules to access. You will then have embraced the miracle of the messages found in this book.

Know that as you read the words of Mother Mary, that you are reading the words of Mother God. If you open your heart to this book, you will feel the Love of these beautiful Divine beings. You will feel the Holy Spirit.

This book is for everyone. It is for people of every

race, every nation, every religion, and every beautiful system of belief.

This book is not to be used solely as a Christian holy book. This is a book about you. For you are an individual part of Father God, Mother God, and the Holy Spirit. That Spirit is the Essence of everything, including you.

Chapter One

We are Angels of the Holy Spirit

All of you indeed are connected, even though you act as individual components of the great Divine Source.

~ Mother Mary, the Holy Spirit

I come to you, not in my own name, but in the name of the Holy Spirit, the Divine Father, and Jesus the Christ. None of us could exist without the blended Oneness of this Grand Trinity that comprises all of existence. The Holy Spirit is who I am and who we all are, and without Her spark of Light beating in our hearts, we could not exist as humans. Embrace Her, the Holy Spirit, and you will embrace yourself.

Yes, I said "Her." I know the Holy Spirit is referred to in many sacred scriptures as He, but my wife and I have spoken with the Holy Spirit, and She is most definitely a beautiful She. She is the Divine Feminine, the Divine Mother, the Great Birther and the Consciousness of the Godhead, throughout all existence.

A Consciousness of Oneness

Everything has a soul, a spirit and thus a consciousness. The Native Americans have always known this. That is why in their traditions, they commune with the spirits of animals, plants, minerals, Earth, sun, sky and water, as well as with other human beings.

Everything on this Earth has a spirit and a consciousness; it is all Spirit, manifested into matter. Everything is made of energy, or Spirit. Spirit is the reality. The concept that all spirits are separate from one another is a misconception. Spirits are all part of one whole Source, and that whole Source is the Holy Spirit.

Though all spirits are part of the Oneness, there is an individual quality to each spirit. Each is an individual component that carries a unique energy signature. We have all been birthed as one of these individual components of the Holy Spirit. On the grand level of higher consciousness, we have never left the Holy Spirit, even though we are having this experience that we call human life. This is the mystery and the paradox: that we are here as humans, as individual spirits, and yet at the same time, are one with the totality of all.

Learning from the Ascended Masters

My wife and I have received direct teachings from the Holy Mother, Jesus and the Holy Father, Saint Joseph, since 2011. Saint Joseph has come to this Earth as many different masterful beings. He is also known in the Grand World of Heaven as Saint Germain, which is the name he goes by in this book.

One of our greatest teachers is Malachi. He is a Grand Teacher, an Ascended Master. Malachi also speaks for the Masterful Angels Zoroaster, Melchizedek, Quan Yin, Buddha, Moses, Jared, Zohar, Kuthumi and many others in the Great White Brotherhood, who are also our teachers.

In our sessions with them, the Ascended Masters and Angels usually speak through or to Malachi, who then relays the messages to us through a channel. Malachi is always with Jesus, the Holy Mother and the Holy Father. Like us, all of these great teachers exist as individual components that are also blended into the One consciousness.

The One, the Holy Spirit, could make this entire holographic world disappear, but chooses not to. She is the same One who has birthed us, gives us life, and who always loves us, Her children. She is the Holy Spirit, Mother God.

She is the One who made a conscious decision to incarnate into the realm of matter here on Earth as the beautiful Mother Mary, the Mother of Jesus. She and Her choice of the Divine Father's representative, Saint Joseph, enlightened this world with the fullness of Light and Spirit.

The Unconditional Love of the Divine Mother

Now allow me to tell you about the Holy Spirit as I perceive Her, when She speaks directly to my wife Marina and me.

She is pure Peace, Unconditional Love, harmony and intellect. She is also pure acceptance, stillness and gentleness. Anything you hear or read that paints the picture of God as a punishing God is not connected to the truth of our beautiful Holy Spirit, the Divine Mother.

People have been taught, brainwashed and persuaded to fear God and to feel guilty for their "sins," and that is not at all what the Divine Mother would like us to think and feel.

For one, She has told us that we are all One with Her, that we are all Divine. Therefore, if we fear God, then we fear ourselves. Secondly, emotions such as fear and guilt are the antithesis of the Divine attributes of faith and Unconditional Love.

It is true that Jesus said, Condemn, and you will be condemned, judge and you will be judged. There do exist Divine laws that operate under the law of cause and effect, or karma. But these are not punishments handed down by the Divine. They are part of a grand design that many of us on a grand level help to create, or co-create.

As Angels of Light and Love, we all very much want to enter this world, this design of free will, where we forget who we are and then have to find our way back to the awareness of who we are.

Do you know who you are?

Every person, every being, has an energy signature. Your energy signature is also who you are as an Angel. Yes, you are an Angel, who for one reason or another decided to leave the beauty and perfection of life on the Other Side and have a lifetime, a human experience, an incarnation upon this Earth.

Who You Really Are

You are an Angel. Can you grasp that? Can you fully believe that? That you, not your body, but you as consciousness, can never die. The consciousness of who you are is eternal. You have a higher awareness beyond what you are now perceiving, for there is much of your consciousness that is hidden from you at this moment.

It's hidden in your subconscious, your DNA, your RNA, your pineal gland, and the parts of the brain that you don't use. Your higher consciousness is hidden in what is ironically called "junk DNA." It is also in the energy systems known as your chakras, in your connection to Source, and in your blended consciousness, which includes the consciousness of all the Ascended Masters, Archangels, Angels and the Oneness of all.

Angels in Human Form

Picture yourself as that Angel, not incarnated anywhere. Picture yourself being excited now that you have the opportunity to walk a golden path. Picture yourself loving God the Source, and know that in Angelic form, you are fully aware that you are one hundred percent part of that Divine Source. Know that you love the Source of who you are, the Source of everything, the great Divine Mother and Father.

You love all of that so much, that you know wholeheartedly that nothing can take that away from you. Nothing can take away the fact of who you really are:

Source consciousness, who is both one with Source, and an individual consciousness within Source, coming out to express your own Divine thought-creations.

You know there is nothing that can separate you from that joy, from the Love, from that Oneness, that happiness, and from all those you call friends. You know that nothing can separate you from all those great Masters, all the great Angels and cosmic beings. You know all of this and you know that you will be born forgetting it all, when you choose the Golden Path. This is to incarnate through your soul, onto the planet Earth, the place of the golden work.

The Amnesia of Earth Life

Before you incarnated into this Earth life, you knew all of the above to be true. But you were warned. You were told that you would forget who you are. You were told that you would forget that you are an Angel.

You were told that you would feel the joy, the Love and the happiness of the higher realms in your younger ages. But that the density of matter, and some of the cruel happenings or hard environments and harsh people around you could and probably would close the doors on most of those memories and realizations.

You were told that you would then maybe be cut off from the awareness of knowing that you are that Source, that you are that Angel that made the conscious decision to have this experience.

Before you got here, you envisioned yourself walking

the earth—healing, teaching, spreading the Light, being full of love, and spreading the word of Source. You envisioned yourself dancing in the rain, swimming beneath the depths of the water, befriending animals, plants and minerals. And loving your fellow humans, your friends, the other Angelic beings who made the same decision you have made.

As an Angel, you may have envisioned all that and said to yourself, how could I not know it, and not find the grace and the glory of the human existence, with this knowingness that I have right now?

How could I not find this Love that existed, this joy that existed in this beautiful Source consciousness, where I know that every other individual energy is part of the One Source, my family of Light? How can that not be when I walk the Earth in matter?

Remembering Who We Are

As we all know, we all did forget who we are to varying degrees, and at times we really have believed that all we were is a human body. We became absorbed in feeding the body's needs, getting it the tools it needs to survive, in the form of money, relationships and material objects. And none of those are bad—don't get me wrong—for we are meant to live in a world of outer abundance.

But when we place the objective of what we want solely in material terms, and do not see the Source consciousness and Source Love of everything, the Source Energy of what we all are, then we miss the point.

We then walk a path of karma, karmic situations of cause and effect. It's fine to have that beautiful car or beautiful house. But know that those things come from Source, and that you are also Source. It's great to give and know that you are giving, because as part of Source Energy, when you're giving, you're giving of God to God.

Perhaps that's why Jesus said when someone takes something from you, don't try to get it back, because it's already in God's hands, and be happy for that. For when you truly know the Source of who you are, the God of who you are, then you always have what you need.

When you have greater awareness, you will learn Divine manifestation, the ability to create the world around you in ways that serve the higher good of everyone. You'll not only have what you need but also what you want, for yourself and for others.

The Christ Consciousness

The beautiful Jesus was born the Christed baby. He was born with a fully activated pineal gland, with awareness of his Christed self. You and I were not. We must learn how to develop that higher consciousness, because it has not come to us naturally.

We can expand into Christ consciousness, first by developing faith in Divine Love, and by releasing worry, fear and doubts. Keeping a heart of discernment, yes, but doubt, worry and fear, no. An expanded awareness tells us when we are in right action, on the right path.

You may be wondering, is my bumpy ride here on Earth the right path? Yes, it is. Can it change for the better? Yes, it can.

Developing Awareness

It can change when you increase your awareness, by knowing who you are, and having the faith to never let that go. In fact, Malachi and Jesus and Saint Germain tell me that it is our fears, doubts and worries that are the Antichrist.

I know when I say the Antichrist, a being comes to mind—a dark, devilish being. In fact, there is no "being." The only real opposition we face is whatever is preventing us from knowing our true Source. It is whatever is preventing us from the awareness that we are Love and Light, the Light of the Divine Source, the Sacred Fire, the Source Consciousness, Divine Love, Divine Harmony, Divine Consciousness—we are all of that.

It is useless to pin the label "Antichrist" on any one person or group. For we all carry doubts and fears on one level or another, until we achieve full Christed awareness. We can dissolve our fears, worries, doubts and judgments, dissolve them into the little white lights of energy that they are, back into Divine Consciousness.

Releasing Our Darker Aspect

Divine Energy has been playing a part in this illusion we call life on Earth, and it's the same with the ones we call "dark beings" on this planet. When we are finished with our worries, fears, doubts and judgments, then the dark ones will finish playing their parts, for they are also Source consciousness. At heart, they are also Divine Beings.

Should they choose not to stop playing the role of dark beings, then as time goes on, when enough of us become aware of our Christed Beingness, our Oneness, then they will no longer be able to vibrate their darkness into action on this beautiful planet Earth.

This is already beginning as I write this in 2013. Those who have played the role of dark beings, who are addicted to the power and the wealth, are losing the power, and losing some of the wealth, so it will happen over time. There is no exact date. It's up to us, Malachi has told us, to be part of the two-thirds of humanity who create the great gateway to the fifth dimension.

It's ironic how two-thirds break down to .666. That number represents the great gateway. We will either continue being controlled by the dark ones on this planet, or decide to live here as Heaven on Earth, as Christed beings, with full awareness of the beautiful Angels we all are.

Even as I write this, two-thirds or .666 of humanity is waking up to the Love, Light and Peace of Divinity. To forgiveness, Unconditional Love, compassion and total awareness that there is no separation between people, nations or beliefs, that all is One.

Once we have achieved this, then Heaven on Earth will truly begin. Then those whose consciousness reflects the Light and Love of Christed consciousness will be the majority of those who are manifesting in this world. We will manifest the beauty, peace and abundance of Heaven and Source consciousness embodied for everyone and everything on this planet. Then the Divine dance, to the Divine symphony, will begin its performance in this beautiful theater we call Earth.

The following chapters contain transcripts of conversations Marina and I have had with Malachi and the Great White Brotherhood of Light. The transcripts relay the actual words of Malachi and the Divine Mother, who is also the Holy Spirit.

Chapter Two

A Radiance of Miracles

That which you are feeling as you heard the Holy Mother—it is a miraculous feeling. It is a radiance of miracles.

- Malachi

From Session L68 6.25.13 — Mother Mary, the Holy Spirit

Malachi: *All right, beautiful beings. We are all here and present, and we as always say, greetings. And as always, [we] ask for the deep breath within yourselves. And as this day you feel the deep breath, feel the blessings of all. And as you are feeling the blessings, do indeed know that we are aware that you have called Mother Mary forward, and to be aware that Her presence is here.*

Now, beautiful ones, you have called a very special Energy forward to greet yourselves. And as you will receive Her, we will ask you to feel the deep Love that is emanated by Her vibration.

For here in your world, you call Her Mother Mary. And here in the Grand World [of Heaven], She is the Holy Spirit.

So we ask you to realize the beauty and the depth of Holy Spirit, as She brings herself forward through this vehicle.

I was shocked to hear Malachi say this. I had planned on asking Mother Mary questions about Her life with Jesus and Saint Joseph. Then in the last few seconds before Mother Mary begins to speak through the Oracle, Malachi tells my wife and me that Mother Mary is the Holy Spirit!

Malachi had taught us previously that the Holy Spirit is the Divine Feminine, the Divine Mother, or Mother God. In the transcript below, my wife and I speak with Mother Mary, channeled through the Oracle.

Mother Mary, the Holy Spirit: *My children, I greet you.*

Kevin and Marina: Greetings, Mother Mary.

Mother Mary, the Holy Spirit: *I ask you to feel the Light around you. In your hearts, you have called me forward. Know [that] in the heart of the Universe, we have called you forward.*

This is a blessed time in your human endeavors. You are aware of the evolution of this time. We ask you, as you breathe with us, to feel us, for in the present moment, we are working with your brain.

The network of the universal consciousness is impressing vibrations through your brain, that you may receive our thoughts. Imprinting vibrations throughout your whole being, that your mind and hearts will find such a unification, that you hear beyond your ears, feel beyond your human heart, know beyond your human endeavors.

We have called you to be agents of Light, spiritual trackers, that through your sacred hearts, you share with your beautiful siblings of life the joy of Spirit, the blessings of Love, the purity of Oneness—the vibrations that have been emitted into your brain.

When the Holy Spirit mentions the evolution of this time, She is referring to the new eon, the New World that we entered in December 2012. She knows that we are aware of the immense Divine Light that is flowing through and around this planet, and through and around our bodies at this time. She knows that we are aware of this Divine loving process, which will eventually bring us into Heaven on Earth, and the thousand years of Peace referred to in scripture.

I asked Malachi about the thousand years of Peace, and he has told us that is how many years it will take for Peace to anchor into this planet, so that it will last forever.

The session continues:

Mother Mary, the Holy Spirit: *We ask you now, to feel the filtering sensation of energy moving through your entire body. We ask of you to place your hand, left hand of your human body, over your heart. With your right hand, let it be open and extended to the collective field of your world.*

As you feel the Love of Peace radiating through you, through your heart, through your hands, recognize the blessing filling you, the blessing released to all.

I give to you this time, that you may ask questions.

Marina and I each placed our left hand over our heart, and extended our right hand out, sending beautiful loving energy out to all of humanity.

The session continues:

Kevin: Thank you, it's very beautiful that we can receive a gift from You, and then give it to humanity at the same time. Can you explain who You are as the Holy Spirit—what that actually means?

Mother Mary, the Holy Spirit: *Indeed. In the beauty of life, the Holy Spirit is the essence of [the] Allness that created the force and form of all existence. I am the vibration of Wholeness, Oneness, Light. I am the Spirit of you.*

In your language, holy means pure, Oneness, complete, sacred. I am the Holy Spirit in you. You are Oneness, sacred, loving. Your Spirit is pure. You are the pure expression that I Am. In this moment of communication, you see, you hear a vibration that appears to you to be individual, and it is the Everything. I am Love, pure within you.

I ask you to feel that glow of Love, pure Holy Spirit, within you. As you recognize yourselves as human in form, you journey in My aspect as a pure curious Spirit. The individual form of all life leads consciousness with curiosity—the seeker, the constant seeking to unify. As your Spirit of awareness guides you to unification, you then are aware of Holy Spirit, the pure aspect of yourself, which is I. Is this explanation clear to you?

Malachi, Saint Germain and Jesus have taught Marina and me in many sessions that we are all Spirit in matter. Now I understand that "Spirit" is the Holy Spirit. Mother Mary says here that we all journey in Her aspect as a pure curious spirit. We are all in the illusion of separated form, while the pure essence of us remains to be the Holy Spirit.

In this separated form, we curiously seek the unification of being One with Holy Spirit, not separate. Most people have no idea that they are Holy Spirit, living an individuated experience in a human body and mind that has been programmed to forget the Essence of who we truly are.

Let's go back to our conversation with Mother God, who chose to incarnate as Mother Mary, the Mother of Jesus:

Kevin: It's wonderful and amazing to us to know who You truly are. That we are experiencing You, and that our purpose on this planet is to truly experience You, to bring that Love, that Holy Spirit into our lives, into our interactions. To realize that everybody around us is also the Holy Spirit of You, of Love. And to be honest, I do realize it, and now I walk the path of attempting to live it.

Mother Mary, the Holy Spirit: *Know within yourselves that [that] which you call an "attempt" is a recognizable action. You are activated to the I Am Presence, the Holy Spirit within you. In the beauty and joy of your essence, you are awakened to the call of your individual selves to remember, in the beauty of Oneness, your quality of living.*

The Oneness state of Love allows your inner consciousness and your outer living to blend in this Oneness. As you allow yourselves the feeling in the field of Oneness in this very moment, you feel as the Being of Oneness within your consciousness, within your Beingness. You feel this unification of energy.

We are aware that you are utilizing the mechanics of human endeavor to see My use forward thrust through an individual body. Yet, in the essence of your own being, that individual quality of your humanness, you feel the Holy Spirit talking within you. You feel the Love emanating. It is within you. You are feeling the unification in the field of your being, in the field of Oneness.

As you spoke, you said, "I am trying to live this." Feel this unification, and you will know you are living it, that you are living the evolution of awareness in the beautiful field of human experience. You are allowing your cellular memory to recall Holy Spirit, to live Holy Spirit, to love Holy Spirit. [Pause]

Can you feel the beauty of the Love in your heart and your mind? Can you feel the exchanges of energy maneuvering your brain to be more open to the vibration of higher consciousness? That you are not only hearing words, spoken through this vehicle, but receiving more? Can you feel this?

Kevin: Yes. I feel it very much. [To Marina] What about you?

Marina: Yes. I feel it too, thank you.

Kevin: I feel a great Love. I feel vibrations in my brain, in my head.

Marina: Opening and expanding my pineal gland.

Kevin: I feel like we've just met our Mother whom we haven't seen in a very long time.

Mother Mary, the Holy Spirit: *And so it is. Let yourselves, in the essence of matter, feel upon your hands, the hand that I extend to you, to let yourselves know that I touch with an embrace to you, the hands that walk with you, through your human endeavors. The hand of guidance, the hand of assurance, the hand, of course and always, of Love.*

Whenever your human experience leaves your mind within the impression of separation, feel your hands being touched by My hand. You will feel the loving guidance assuring you, for there is much your soul of individuality has accepted to learn, to help support the beauty of the human endeavor, [now] focusing on the evolution of Oneness.

When Mother Mary asked me to feel Her hand, I was astonished. I often feel the energy of the Angels and Ascended Masters, but Her energy is noticeably different. It feels as if the palms of my hands had a magnetic charge to them, and She is taking a magnet and playfully and gently moving it about across my palms, pulling at them.

She offers that we can call upon Her, so that we can feel Her when we begin to get caught up in our human challenges, when we feel separate from Holy Spirit and Oneness. I have been practicing this form of contact every day. I open my hands so that my fingers are pointing almost straight up and my palms are open to the air and this Divine experience.

To try this exercise, ask Mother Mary, the Holy Spirit, to extend to you Her loving Divine touch, because you are also Her beautiful child. Be patient, because you may have to learn to be sensitive to feeling energy. Also have faith, because doubt will interfere even with the Holy Spirit, because of Divine law of free will, which She abides by as well. I've prayed to Holy Spirit that She will energize these words so you can have a much better chance of experiencing Her loving, sometimes playful touches.

The session continues:

Mother Mary, the Holy Spirit: *In the aspect of the human endeavor, the more you know of the purity of your Holy Spirit, the less you will feel the separation or the mission of your soul, a soul on a lonely journey. The more you feel your Oneness, the more there is no worry. Peace prevails in your mind, in your endeavors.*

In your mission, you will share wisdom, teaching individual components how to Love in Oneness, how to feel unification, how to delight in individual expression. And yet always knowing [that] there is no separation.

These Divine words are full of the answers to the great mystery of why we are here on Earth, and our soul purpose. The Divine Mother is saying that the more we understand and live within the Holy Spirit, the more the mission of our soul can evolve.

It is the mission of our souls to get us to realize our Spirit self, our connection to Holy Spirit, and the Oneness that we all share. For almost everyone, this mission of the soul continues for our entire life, and into many other Earth lives.

When you live in enlightenment, knowing and realizing that you are Light, that you are Spirit in matter, and come to the actualization that the Spirit of who you are is pure Love and pure intelligence, then the mission of the soul changes to a mission of service. Service of spreading the message of Light and Peace. And as Mother Mary said, of assisting people in understanding Oneness, without separation.

We are not locked into karmic patterns of happiness followed by sadness, joy followed by suffering, stability followed by chaos. We can free ourselves, free the soul from that endless cycle. To do this, you must ask yourself, Am I finally finished with the ups and downs of life, and ready to commit to unconditional Peace? Am I finally ready to feel Peace and Harmony, and be an encouraging example to others?

The session continues:

Mother Mary, the Holy Spirit: *Into your world, in [the] evolution of consciousness, the human endeavor initiated separation. Yet always in your minds, always in your hearts, the impulse to know your Divinity has prompted every soul to evolve to the recall[ing] of the Oneness.*

In the evolutionary states, there has been names given to the Oneness. This day you have called the Oneness forward as Mother Mary, for in the time of your evolution, you have known of the Holy Spirit as the Birther of Life, as the Holy Mary the Mother of Life, [who] to many of you has been known as the Birther of the One named Jesus, [Spanish pronunciation] *Jesus, Yahweh, Yeshua.*

Here the Holy Spirit is referring to the first Golden

Age, when human beings were able to live in body yet still be aware of their overall Oneness.

The beautiful Garden of Eden, in the story of Genesis, is a symbol of Oneness, when humankind lived in awareness of its Oneness, with all the members of its race and all of creation, and the Divine. The "temptation" offered by the serpent in the Garden of Eden is a symbol of the lower mind and ego, the individual desire that created the belief in separateness over Oneness. When that occurred, then guilt, suspicion, fear and service-to-self prevailed, creating even further separation.

From what I have learned from the Divine Mother, the Divine Father, Jesus and Malachi, it is not sexual relations (or "original sin") that separate one from experiencing Oneness with the Divine. The belief in our individual separateness—from Creator, and from one another—occurs when we fail to see the Divine in everything. Everything we touch, see, feel and experience on this Earth.

There is great beauty in the quality of innocence that flows from the nature of Divinity, and that innocence extends to our sexuality as well. In one of our sessions, Malachi made a very strong statement about celibacy. He said that we cannot find enlightenment or Oneness through celibacy, only further separation from Oneness.

The Holy Spirit goes on to tell us that even though we choose to have a consciousness of separateness, we have always carried the impulse to know the One God, the Source, and the Holy Spirit.

We have given thousands of names over thousands of years to the Oneness of all. There is one name for the Divine that the Divine Mother uses to name Herself in this session, which most of the Divine Angels have also used, and that is "I AM" or "I Am That I Am."

Jesus also said, "I Am the Light of this World" or "I Am the Way, the Truth and the Life." The "I Am" is not simply a reference to "I" as in "just me." It is a reference to Oneness. The "I Am" is the Universe; it is all of us, and All That Is.

In this session, Mother God explains that my perception of a separate "Her" speaking to a separate "me" is really an illusion. In the ultimate reality, we are all One with God, the I Am. Is the Divine Mother actually speaking to us? Yes, She is. But we are all a part of who She is, though we have imagined ourselves to be separate from Her Essence.

When we realize that there can be no separateness, that the presence of the Mother is inside all of us, then we can utilize that "I AM Presence" ourselves. You and I can then say, "I AM the Light of this world!" We may not quite believe it at first, because we may view ourselves in terms of our human imperfections. But in that moment, we are activating the Divine consciousness, just by saying, "I AM!"

If we can continue to say, "I AM the Light of this world," especially if we say it with more and more positive intention every day, we begin to see a change in ourselves and our outer lives. We will soon be living a higher consciousness, experiencing more Love and Light than we could ever have thought possible.

The session continues:

Mother Mary, the Holy Spirit: *And as the learned ones know, the name of such Master was given as Christed. Christ, the contained essence of the re-generated Source, the I AM presence in the signature of the human form. A model for humanity to follow, that the human form of consciousness could utilize an awareness of potential within themselves.*

For the One, my Son, noted to the world as Jesus, the Christed One, presented a formation in the human design to reveal to all the power of Love, within the beauty of the frequency of Love, the power of Peace, and healing in the power of unification, that Jesus the Man could display to humanity much [that] was being learned.

To the humans, it was mystery, and what your world today calls "magic." For the questions were always, how does He do this?

The Holy Spirit Mother Mary is the Mother of all existence, as well as the biological Mother of Jesus the Christ. Christ is not a name, but a state of higher consciousness. It is the *Christos,* the crystalline (Light body) consciousness.

The Divine Mother calls the Holy Spirit the regenerated Source—the Holy Spirit Essence that is reborn into the contained essence that is human form. She tells us that the I Am presence, when understood and utilized, can create harmony, healing, unification and knowledge of the pure essence of all, which is Peace and Love.

Our Mother describes how Her Son Jesus came to be an example of the Christed being, so that all of humanity could realize that the potential of being a Christ is there for everyone. She states how humanity marvels at how Jesus created miracles. During our last one hundred or more sessions, Jesus, Malachi, Saint Germain and many other Masters have been revealing to us how Jesus did what He did.

(Successive books will reveal all of this information. These will include *Jesus, the Greatest Healer; Jesus, the Prince of Peace; The Sacred Life of Joseph; Manifestation and Master Consciousness; The New Human Template for a New Age*; and *The Book of Malachi.*)

The session continues:

Mother Mary, the Holy Spirit: *Unto yourselves, you are learning how this Son, called Jesus, did this. He merged his human awareness with the essence of Holy Spirit, Divine Oneness. As any of you Sons and Daughters of the Holy Spirit align in such presence within your consciousness, you become humble Oneness. You come to the space within your sacredness that holds no question, simply the Beingness of the desired vibration that becomes an outcome in the realm of your matter.*

Here the beautiful Holy Mother is saying that we can all do what Jesus did, and gives us a hint about how he did it. She mentions that Marina and I are learning how Jesus worked what we call miracles. We have been taught numerous lessons by the Great Masters, including Jesus. They have taught us to merge with Holy Spirit, which they also call the thirteenth dimension.

The Divine Mother says that we can experience "humble Oneness" in which we free ourselves from the lower ego and move our conscious focus to our higher self and to our heart-mind. In those moments, we surrender our ego completely, that part of ourselves that constantly speaks out in a declaration of separateness.

We surrender to Holy Spirit by realizing our Oneness with all that it is.

From this blended state of consciousness, we then can bring this Divine energy into our Earthly body and the material realm, charging the field within and around us with positive attributes of the Divine. This is how manifestation works. It focuses on charging your field of emotion, field of energy and field of energetic photons with the feelings and states of consciousness that you want to attract into your life.

In contrast, when we operate solely in the realm of matter, then we are bound by the Earthly laws of physics, for the most part. But when we bring our consciousness up into the realm of the Holy Spirit, the realm of the Divine, then we're operating with all the possibilities of Divinity. This is Divine Manifestation, and it is something we can all learn to do.

Mother Mary, the Holy Spirit has told us, "I did not birth only one Child to perform in the realm of matter what is seen as miracle. I have birthed all to be the miraculous reality of Oneness." Allow yourselves to be the miraculous Holy Spirit!

Holy Spirit is inviting us to *be* Holy Spirit. This is what Oneness is all about. We don't have to worry that when we blend into the Oneness, we will lose ourselves. Instead, we come more fully into our best and brightest selves, as we become a commander of Holy Spirit in this Earth realm.

Though we still have far to go in the realm of the Divine, we can actively operate from within the presence of Holy Spirit that is within us. When we master this, then we are able to manifest freely on this Earth all of the abundance, Love, Peace and fulfillment we have dreamed of having, in their highest form.

One of the major steps we must climb in order to reach this point is to master Peace in our own lives. Peace is the path to Love and the path to God. We must resonate with the vibration of Divine Peace in order to truly blend with the Holy Spirit. There is no exception. We must commit to Peace in every way in our own being—in our personal life, family life, relationships, business dealings and community life. We cannot show support for any war and be committed to Peace. We must embody Peace itself.

The session continues:

Malachi: [Chuckles] *All right, beautiful beings. You have been blessed by Her presence, have you not?*

Kevin: So incredible! Yes.

Marina: Thank you so much.

Malachi: *Now, we always ask you, how do you feel? Do we not? We ask you that now with the depth of yourselves, what do you recognize in the cellular feeling of your being?*

Kevin: I feel a joyful excitement, a great realization, and an amazing absorption of who She is. Because I am here in this body, and to know that what everybody has been reaching for, for all these thousands and thousands of years is Her, that Holy Spirit, the Love, the Oneness—

Malachi: *Indeed. Indeed, it is.*

Kevin: —which we are all part of.

Malachi: *You are blessed by the greatest blessing, the Unconditional Love of the Holy Spirit. Beautiful woman, how are you feeling?*

Marina: At first, I felt very grateful for this pleasure to meet the Holy Spirit, and to feel a great Love, and I still feel it in my body. I'm very thankful to Mother Mary for helping me to recognize that, that vibration of great Love.

Now I want to make my goal to feel Her essence in every

human being, so I can radiate that Love for everybody. That's what I want to learn—how to live that life. I'm very thankful to Her for that gift of beautiful energy, and I'm very excited, I'm very happy.

I still feel that energy vibrating in my heart and my whole body. It's almost like my body is a sponge that absorbs that energy so greatly, and it just feels absolutely wonderful. Thank you so much, to Mother Mary, to Malachi, and to the Oracle.

Malachi: *You have felt the greatest Unification.*

Marina: Yes, we have!

Malachi: [Chuckles] *And with it, as you know, you will radiate this. It will continue its flow through you, and you will radiate it in this collective field. And that is a beautiful blessing, a blessing of the Divine self, indeed.*

And beautiful ones, that which you are feeling as you heard this beauty of the Holy Mother—it is a miraculous feeling. If it is a miraculous feeling, then comprehend [that] it is a radiance of miracles. Allow yourselves throughout this time and space of your existence of feeling, to indeed lend into feeling your Love Unconditional, to spread the vibration to all of your humanity.

Now, before it is the time [for me] to leave the human body, do you have a question here?

Kevin: One thing that confused me—not about this session, but in the last session with Mother Mary, that period of time keeps coming up, of 2,600 years. Because our calendar says that the life of Jesus occurred around 2,000 years ago.

Malachi: *Here, beautiful one, let us speak in the manner that perhaps the confusion will ease in your mind-thinking, shall we do that?*

Into what is called your histories, yes, you say a bit more than 2,000 years [ago], was the birthing and the existence of Jesus the Man, do you not? And here you have heard us speak of 2,600 [years]—why? Well, let's have you think about what we have been calling unto yourselves, [which] is to be aware of a New Garden, do you understand? And to be aware that the Garden is being cultivated.

Cultivated so that what materializes in your world is the true essence of your shimmering consciousness, the beauty of pure Peace and harmony, the expression of pure Love. So you go to 2,600 years, and you'll say there was the impregnation, the planting of a New Garden. And you will realize that in the human time endeavor, it took quite a number of years before Jesus the Man could birth into that Garden. Do you understand?

The Divine Plan to bring a Christed One into the world was part of this cultivation of the New Garden. The family that almost 600 years later would give birth to Mary and Joseph was being seeded. The Holy Mother Mary and the Holy Father Joseph were both born into sacred families.

In another session, Malachi spoke to us regarding the lineage of Mary:

Holy Mother Mary, and her parentage as well—they were taught that the sacredness of walking upon the Earth was extremely important to honor. That every footstep that they took upon the Earth was a graciousness of the Divine creation. And again, the power of Light, and the power of Love, and the power to be One with all Nature, was important. So whether it was a seed, [the] plant world, or the beauty of the animal world, or the Nature spirit of the human consciousness, all was held in sacred regard.

The session continues:

Kevin: Does that time, of 2,600 years ago, coincide with the beginning of the Piscean era?

Malachi: *Indeed, indeed. Now you're in new era, are you not?*

Kevin: We are on the cusp of Aquarius, aren't we?

Malachi: *Indeed, you are. You're in truly a new eon. And in the value of this state of conscious time, we encourage you to continue to know that you are cultivating a Garden. And [that] the preparation is occurring within yourselves that does birth the true Christed being, of your own individual qualities. Do you understand?*

Notice that Malachi is saying we will all eventually become Christ-like. The Garden that is being cultivated is a Garden of growing and rapidly expanding human consciousness. When our collective human consciousness grows and expands beyond the confines of the lower ego, then we will pierce the veil that currently separates the dimensions of consciousness. We will then be in the fifth dimension. (As I write this, Earth's people are quickly ascending into the fourth dimension.)

It is up to the desire and mission of each soul as to whether it will decide to make the leap with the rest of humanity into the new world of the fifth dimension, or remain in lower states of consciousness. If a soul prefers to remain in third-dimensional consciousness, then it is blessed and given a world or environment in which to play out that experience. It will not be anywhere on the beautiful, new, loving Mother Earth, where we are beginning even now to experience the first phases of Heaven on Earth.

You may be asking how we will go from our current state of consciousness to Heaven on Earth. In stages, we will go from war, crime, despair, poverty, pollution and white collar corruption—one aspect of Holy Spirit trying to destroy another aspect of Holy Spirit—to living at Peace with one another, our Earth and ourselves.

It is accomplished one soul at a time. Each of us, one at a time, can awaken to the illusion of the belief that we are separate—and see that when we are harming another, we are really harming ourselves.

The New World will come about as each of us, one by one, commits to being in a state of Peace that is unconditional. Join us, because we truly are inheriting this beautiful Earth, and there will be one thousand years of Peace, then Peace for eternity upon this future land of joy.

In this new eon, we are no longer alone, because the great Divine Beings are with us now in a very tangible way, as you have learned just by reading this book. Can you imagine their patience, as they planted the seeds for the birth of Jesus the Christ 2,600 years ago? Jesus Himself planted the seeds for the future birth of and awakening of many Christed beings. We can each become a Christed being if we choose, if we are willing to follow the path.

This is not a path of guilt and sin, pain and punishment, of belief in separateness, or of holy wars. It is a path of Love and Peace. This is a path of realization and awareness of the truth that you are a beautiful shining Angel who excitedly incarnated into this world of duality, to witness this great event, of the ascension of an entire planet into a higher dimension. Your higher self, your spirit self, is an Angel and part of Holy Spirit, Mother God, the Spirit of all existence and all perfection. You hold Her power, glory, grace, intellect, creativity, Love, purity, and Peace within you; now is the time for you to fully live it.

Jesus did not come to the Earth as an example of a Christed being so he could be worshiped and kept high on a pedestal. He came to blaze the path for you and me, to tell us that we can live as He lived.

He still holds the torch of that life, so that we can find our way through the darkness whenever we fall off the enlightened path. For He and the Holy Spirit do not judge and punish those who stumble on the path and live by the dictates of the demons of the lower ego. Jesus and all of the Divine Masters and Angels are ever-present, to offer the hand of Light and Love and the hand of the Holy Spirit, whom they are One with.

They are here to help us, and there are no exceptions regarding who we are or what we have done. They cannot be deceived, because they see through the façade of those who are controlled by the lower ego. They also see and will forever remind us of the beauty of the Angel and the soul that are active within all of us.

The session continues:

Malachi: *Unto yourselves, you are applying the knowledge—the knowledge of being a Christed One, a Master. You are imprinting it in your own dynamic cellular memory of your soul, and you are imprinting this in the beautiful cellular memory of the collective field of humanity.*

As each of you willing to live the Christed mastership of consciousness remind yourselves, you are preparing the Earth's peoples, souls that will enter the Earth again and again, to indeed come to such a Master state of consciousness.

Till the Garden well! Cultivate its seeds well. And as we often say, worry not, do not over-concern yourselves that you have not perfected this purity of consciousness. Allow its evolution. Do you understand?

Malachi is saying here that we are all students of Christed consciousness. When we bring ourselves into that state of consciousness, we create a ripple effect that is felt by the human collective.

He is also letting us all know that this process of the Earth becoming Heaven on Earth will take at least a couple of generations. There will be an increasing consciousness that will be noticeable during this time, so that every couple of years, you can look back at your own life and events that have occurred on the Earth, and see changes that for most people will represent an increase in consciousness and a decrease in the dualistic illusions of the third dimension.

Malachi also suggests using patience as we walk the path of Christed consciousness. He is also suggesting that we enjoy the journey.

The session continues:

Malachi: *And is there yet another question?*

Kevin: Can I ask about the other children in Mother Mary's

life? I don't know all of their names, but I'm guessing, Jude, Simon and James, though I don't know if James was her child by Joseph. I believe there were also some daughters, maybe two or three—Ruth and a couple of other girls. We all carry a Christed essence, but did they carry Christed awareness?

Malachi: *Very good, very good. Beautiful one, as the Man that was called Jesus was the essence of consciousness that came forth in the soul expression on the Earth, already mastering through the soul vibration with an intention to be the leader of Masters, then you would say that the One that was called Jesus of Her children, as that of the Virgin Mother Mary, was the One that came forward with the greater aspect of living Christed awareness.*

That which would be called the 'human children' that She brought forth during that era contained within themselves the potentiality for that Christed consciousness. They did choose to be what your world would call more of the students of Jesus. And the reason [is], [that] as Jesus was to say to humanity, "Here is the way," they were saying unto humanity, "Here is the way to learn."

And so, yes—did they have the capability? Indeed. Yet their service was to implore the individuals to comprehend how to study, how to practice, how to evaluate, and how to live.

Here you will say to yourselves, you are Her children. How are you learning, and how are you living the Christed awareness? As She did tell you, it is miraculous consciousness, is it not?

Malachi is confirming for us here that in Her human form, Mary did birth other children into their family. The other children assisted Jesus and assisted others about how to learn from Jesus. Malachi wants us all to know that we are the children of the Holy Spirit, the Holy Mother. And we all have the ability to live with Christed awareness, and develop the ability to create miracles He performed.

Malachi went on to say, "And so you will say [that] you are Her children; you are cultivating miraculous consciousness."

Here Malachi is letting us know that we are being taught the sacred knowledge. We are students of Christed awareness, students of Jesus, Malachi, Saint Germain, the Divine Mother and other Great Masters. My wife Marina and I made the commitment, both before we entered this life and now, to be students of the Divine Mysteries, to live a sacred life, and to pass the knowledge of the Divine gifts to everyone who will receive them.

The session continues:

Malachi: [Chuckling] *You are good students.*

Kevin: Thank you, we are very happy about that.

Marina: Very happy.

Malachi: *All right, beautiful beings, once again we desire to allow you to spend some time simply feeling the beautiful essence of Her presence, the Holy Spirit of Love within you. Therefore, we will leave the body, and as always, we ask you to take up the blessings. Peace be with you.*

Kevin and Marina: Thank you, Malachi.

When I was preparing to ask questions for what was planned to be this session with the Holy Mother Mary, I had no idea that She is the Holy Spirit. I had no idea that Malachi would introduce Her in any other manner than of the Holy Mother, Mother of Jesus the Christ.

I had long felt deep inside that the Divine Mother had blessed the Holy Mother Mary with very high stature in the hierarchy of Heaven, but I was still surprised. What a beautiful and perfect revelation. Now you and I know that the Divine Mother is the Holy Spirit, and that She chose to incarnate into this blessed planet Earth as Mary, to give birth to our beautiful brother Jesus, the Son of God.

I wrote this on June 25, 2013 after meeting Mary for the first time with the understanding of her as Divine Mother:

> Today Marina and I met the Divine Mother, the Holy Spirit, who is Mother God and Holy Mother Mary. My heart is still pulsing with excitement. My cells are vibrating with the Essence of the Holy Spirit. She does desire to see this world in Peace.

> She does desire for all of us to raise our awareness to Christed consciousness. She told us that She did not give birth to just one Christ, but to all of us, and that we all hold the potential to become Christed beings.

Life as a Waking Dream

Most of us live our lives asleep, not knowing that we are dreaming. And in the dream, the illusion, our consciousness believes it is "less than," thus it is open to being controlled. This low self-esteem, this belief that we fall very low in the sacred order of Life, creates a void, a need to have others approve of us and have others be in control of our lives, to treat us as less than, inferior, incapable and limited. It also creates and attracts the opposite in nearly every culture—a group or class of people who desire to be controlling, to treat others as less than, inferior, incapable and limited. It has created a centuries-old class of rulers, tyrants and dictators.

What most people don't realize is that we ourselves created and often continue to give power to those who seek to control us on every level, including government, religion, education, economics—all areas of life. When we change our awareness and our consciousness to the level of knowing that All are holy, All are powerful, and All have created this world, we begin to take our power back, to realize our incredible worth.

When we radiate this awareness, radiate Love and

Peace, we have a great effect upon the human collective. One by one, each of us then contributes to the human collective, no longer creating oppression, but in its place, the Love, Peace and equality that are based on the equality within the Spirit that we are all a part of.

Disharmony in Our World

What has created the disharmony of our world? Why was it not known and accepted that the Holy Spirit is the Divine Mother, the Divine Feminine, the Great Birther? She births all of creation and is all of creation. She is the great force and form of all existence, as She revealed to us. We were intentionally, purposely deceived—led to believe that God is far away from us, and is angry with us for our lowly human stature. That God requires that we perform certain rituals and follow certain human inventions, such as religion, in order to be acceptable, in order to one day be admitted to heaven. Religion is a great form of social control, used by governments as a form of social and economic manipulation for centuries.

But let us not be angry or bitter toward those people and institutions that deceived us, or perhaps simply had no idea of the truth about the Holy Family and the holy lineage of humankind. Let us maintain in our awareness that those we call the dark ones, those we say deceived us or oppressed us, those we call tyrants, are still us. The Divine Mother has told us, "You are the pure expression that I AM; Love pure, within You."

Can we truly accept that we are a component of God? Part of the Source of all creation? Can we truly accept that we are Creator Beings with abilities to create, like our beautiful Divine Mother and Father? Is humankind finally ready to realize fully that Jesus set a brilliant example of what we all can be—Christed Creator Beings, blended with the Holy Spirit, the Spirit of Wholeness?

A New Age Has Been Birthed

We have entered a new eon of time, in which the Divine Mother is sending loving rays of Light and Divine energy for us to absorb. These energies are helping us to shed the skin of our old self, by renewing and activating our DNA, RNA, chakras and the Divine essence of every cell.

These energies are also working to open up our heart-minds, and the higher mind that connects to the Holy Spirit. Through the heart-mind, we can decipher truth from lies, deception and misinformation from reality. No more secrets. No more lies. Increasingly, they will become impossible for anyone to maintain.

Many of us have spent much of our lives seeking truth, and now that we have found it, we wish to gift it to you. Read with your beautiful heart-mind, and absorb what you have been waiting to hear for so long, for so many lifetimes. Absorb the truth, as we reveal all that is revealed to us.

These writings are from God and the Divine Angels, who have blended completely with the Divine Mother and Father. None of us who transmit Divine teachings are ourselves the bridges between the worlds. Worlds are not separated by time and space. There is no separation, save a conscious awareness of the idea that we are all One. Not separate.

Marina and I gained our conscious awareness by being students of these great Light Beings for more than two years. Our agreement to do this work, which was agreed upon before we were birthed into this incarnation, has enabled us to bridge our human consciousness with Divine consciousness. Otherwise, we are the same as everyone else. Neither we nor our books are to be raised above, nor are the Divine words and wisdom contained within.

Sleeping Gods

These great Divine Beings do not want you to "follow" anyone. They do not want you to worship anyone, other than to show loving devotion to the Divine Mother, the Holy Spirit, and to show devotion to each other and to all that is, because we are all that body of Divinity.

These books are not meant to start any religion or doctrine of thought that draws any line in the sand, that designates yet another "side" or point of view.

The way of these Divine Beings of Light is to recognize the Divinity in all. Because we are, or have been, sleeping gods. All part of the Oneness.

You may reply that other revelations have supposedly occurred, that many before now have written about Divinity and humankind, and that much of what they wrote was not true. I will say that in this era that has now past, most of humanity was sound asleep, believing deeply in the illusion of separateness, that we all exist separately from God and from one another.

Thus the human collective was feeling less than Divine, not worthy to be Divine Spirit in matter. Doctrines of misinformation manifested as a mirror image to the collective consciousness of that third-dimensional Earth time. Any teaching that places Divinity at a distance is false, because it is not teaching that the presence of Source, Divinity and Holy Spirit are all within you.

The Proof

Now, some of you will ask us, where is the proof in all of this? Or, why doesn't Jesus or the Holy Mother just appear and tell us about what is written in these books? Saint Germain has said that you cannot prove anything to another person if they are not ready to accept the truth of it. How could you prove to someone who is blind that a particular object was red or blue? All of your "proof" will be left by the wayside.

The Angels have also confirmed that they do not want to create a "flash in the pan" so that people will be in awe of a Divine Being appearing, and perhaps worship that being, forming religions around that being without truly "getting" that we are *all* Divine, All a part of the Oneness. We are all eternal, just as the Divine is. Our holographic bodies are merely vehicles, made of particles graciously on loan from our beautiful Mother Earth.

Our Divine Oneness, our I Am presence, our Holy Spiritness—the individual components of the Holy Spirit that we are—is all eternal.

Greater Things

We can now know this, live it and actualize it. We can be steadfast on our way to achieving Christ consciousness. Many Christed beings will be amongst us in this century, the first century of this new Golden Age. As Jesus said, "I tell you the truth, anyone who has faith in me will do what I have been doing. He or she will do even greater things than these." [John 14:12] It is time to stop burying the truth of those words, and to finally live them.

This time is here now. Christed Beings are being seeded about the planet, and others will rise from its fertile lands, and from within its hollow body. The seeds are planted, and students of the Christed One, with many of the Divine Beings of Heaven, the Heart of the Holy Spirit, are on the path to Christed awareness. The awareness that we are all Divine Beings, with the presence of God within us. We will come with all different gifts, and the ability to perform many different kinds of miracles.

Do you want to be one of these Christed Beings? Do you feel the urge, the impulse, and the inspiration? Just ask, and you shall be set in motion. Study our books, because every lesson that the Masters have bestowed upon us will be shared in our books. We will also be releasing *Lessons of Enlightenment*, which will contain all of the lessons, meditations and exercises that the beautiful Ascended Masters and the Archangels have graced upon us.

Commit to your study. Commit to your practices, and commit to being aware of your I AM presence, the Holy Spirit operating within you.

The Divine Mother wants you, the holy Angels want you, and we want you. Stay on your path, and an Angel will contact you. Your day has come.

Chapter Three

Hiding the Truth of Mary's Identity

Now we are going to explain what is called the consciousness of humanity. And how the covering up has occurred.

~ Malachi

From Session L69 6.24.13 — The Holy Spirit:

This session occurred the day after the last session, when the Holy Spirit spoke directly to us:

Kevin: Based on yesterday's session, on what was revealed, it seems to me that you may want to call the hiding of Mother Mary's identity the greatest covering up of the truth that has ever been achieved, at least in our eon, that we know about. I am referring to the covering up that took place after Jesus, Mary and Joseph lived, in human form. And I think even the covering up is covered up. [All laugh]

The controlling powers of the world, some of those in power, at least at the present time, seem to know a lot of this information already, and have kept it from people. So some may have known in the past as well, that Mary was, or is, the Holy Spirit, the Divine Mother, right?

Malachi: *Indeed.*

Kevin: So they knew this information, about Mary's true identity, and wanted to hide it from humanity. I believe Jerusalem was burned down about 70 CE, and the Library of Alexandria was burned down as well.

Malachi: *Indeed.*

Kevin: And I read in the Edgar Cayce readings that Ruth, the daughter of Mary and Joseph, married a man who worked in government, and that he actually went to Greece, to the Library of Alexandria and the temple there, the Alexandrian Serapeum, to bring writings about Jesus to those libraries, and secure them there.

[**Author's note:** I know some believe the Library of Alexandria was burned down before the time of Jesus, but scholars say there were several acts of destruction that occurred at different times. The above information I derived from the Edgar Cayce readings.]

So maybe that's one reason why that library was burned down, and why Jerusalem was burned down in 70 CE, to try to destroy evidence of Mary's identity in early Christian writings.

Marina: Didn't they also try to create disharmony about female energy, to try to bring women down, which led to an imbalance in human life, an imbalance between the masculine and feminine energies? Which led to more destruction—the creation of more wars, because people lived without having a positive sense of feminine energy, the Mother energy that's so much more nurturing—?

Malachi: *Indeed! All right—*

Kevin: I have one more to add to that—[laughs]

Malachi: *Indeed.*

Kevin: Adding to what Marina said, the Church has called God 'Father, Son and Holy Spirit,' or 'Father, Son and Holy Ghost,' which you hear less often now. But they never recognize Father, Son and Mother. They never give credit to the Holy Spirit for being the Divine Mother.

Malachi: *Indeed.*

Kevin: So they've retained that part of the covering up. And now, please speak. We are finished! [All laugh]

Malachi: *All right. Now, beautiful ones, we are going to explain what is called the consciousness of humanity, and how the covering up [of Mary's identity] has occurred. Then we will add to that the beauty of evolution of the universal consciousness. Do you understand?*

Kevin: Yes.

Malachi: *In what you could term the most ancient of your times of learning and feeling, and what you in your world would even call intuiting the connection of the Divine, then your humanity did indeed know that the Holy Spirit was the Divine Feminine, birthing the energies into individual Beingness.*

In the evolution of humanity, through the process that we have called the process of separation, the more humanity continued to feel the dynamics of only humanness, their third-dimensional reality, the less they could comprehend the grander aspect of the Divine Feminine and the Divine Masculine.

As the times, and we will call them the eons of times, were occurring, then there became that fallacy, we'll call it fallacy, that there was the separation of masculine and feminine.

And as was noticeable in the human form, the masculine body carried a great deal more physical muscular strength then the feminine body. The feminine body, to the humans, became a very strange mystery. Why? Well, because it was popping out babies! Do you understand? [All laugh]

And in the beginning of the consciousness of humanity, there was not the realization of how the babies were even being created. And so the Woman became a fearful thing, do you understand? Indeed!

And of course, you [now] have great knowledge of the workings of the temple of the human body, and the gift of the masculine and the feminine to bring forth babies into the world. But realize [that] there was a time on this Earth when that was not knowable reality. As the feminine was to be feared, and the masculine had such physical strength, then there was the bowing to the masculine, that they were to be in charge, and to control the feminine, the fearful aspect.

Now have a good giggle. Do you not find a humanity trying to control everything they fear?

Kevin: Yes.

Now you have the indication of how that began to evolve itself, do you not?

As time went forward, beautiful one, there came a time in which the division began to be even stronger between masculine and feminine—and to some religions, there was always the holding [as] holy both qualities.

Then the separation began, truly came during what you could call the era of the strength of [the] Hebrews. For which and unto they brought into this world a belief, that there could be seen only one aspect, and unto them, they indeed made that aspect masculine.

Then, beautiful one, over time, as the human endeavor continued its separation from its Spirit Beingness, then became more of what you call "controlling factors." Controlling factors—religious heads, and eventually government heads.

For a while, beautiful one, on your human force field, your religious and governmental heads were one and the same.

As that was so, then there began what was called the full use of the lower ego, and in the use of the lower ego began then the endeavors of, "How do I stay in my masterful position, and keep others from becoming as masterful?"

Then you had more conflicts, and you had more edicts that were coming from that, whether it be [from] the priests, the head of the religious belief systems, or the heads of governments.

And as time has gone by, that has strongly remained, until the spark of the Divine initiated that evolutionary separation to begin its course of turning back into Union.

Now, let us speak of another reality for you. As in all things that come into the realms of matter or individualization, in the evolutionary power, it must have what is termed in your world [as] that of the yin and the yang, the masculine and the feminine, the active and the passive energy fields.

Within that then, there is also what is built in cycles. How [can] you compare your cycles—well, all of you on the Earth can compare it right to your Nature, for you have summer, you have fall, you have winter, you have spring. Those are called cycles, are they not?

You have cycles of your weather patterns. You have cycles of your thought patterns, and your emotional patterns. And you have cycles of living and dying. In the patterning of the Grand Universe, there are also cycles, in which there has been a grander influence of a feminine [cycling], and then a grander influence of a masculine cycling.

So now, let us take you back to when eon times are in their change. It is during that point, that that Divine Feminine, that Holy Spirit of the Feminine, comes forward more strongly. For it is birthing a new reality, and it is nurturing that new reality. It is indeed impregnating the thoughts and the emotional patterns within all of it, to grow and to develop.

Now, we oftentimes utilize what you would call the parenting of children. And there is the time in which the child is birthed, and it is nurtured to learn how to feed itself, how to clothe itself, how to evolve, involve and evolve itself in its natural cycles of its living.

And then there comes a time in which the child is set free to use its own knowledge. Well, that is the time when it is gone from its feminine trend into its masculine trend. Do you understand? And so you see that also in cycles.

For a great period of time, there was only that known unto the human force field, as this mysterious feminine. And then there was a paradigm shift, and it became more of the masculine to put into action all that is beautiful, and [that] the Divine Feminine had brought forth and birthed forth. In the cycle of your incarnation, you have been blessed to see an eon change, have you not?

And its lead is that of the feminine once again. A birthing, with the greatest intention in this cycle of the newness, to bring the balance of the masculine and the feminine forward. Unto yourselves, you can call it the God and the Goddess if you will.

Into your human endeavors and of your own selves, you have watched this develop. You have found where the women are not so mysterious, and have taken positions strongly in alignment with the male as well.

And the male has allowed themselves to come into a greater balance within their own consciousness. They don't have to be a force field all the time. So you'll say there have been cycles and phases of paradigms.

Now, why did they hide the feminine under that ruling that became only the masculine? And why did they hide the vibration of Mary, the incarnation of the Holy Spirit? Why did they hide the vibration of Jesus as a Christed consciousness?

For humanity simply named Him "Jesus Christ." They were not even aware of the terminology of the word Christ ["anointed one"], were they beautiful ones? As though this was His name, not a state of consciousness.

And Joseph, indeed, given away to hide in the background, and saying unto the world, "Well, here this one, Mary, was a virgin, having a baby that the Holy Spirit conceived." Well, now you'll have a good giggle in your heart. [Kevin laughs]

Malachi: *Indeed. She did conceive, did she not?*

Kevin: Yes!

Malachi: *And in the realm of matter She utilized the vibration of that which was the embodiment of the feminine and that [of] Joseph, which was the embodiment of the masculine. But humanity construed it differently. Why?*

Again, because humanity was working through a masculine paradigm, and believing that the masculine was in charge, and that here this woman could not have had a sacred child with only a human being. And so was also the attitude, that human beings were less than Source. Do you understand?

I want to stop and recognize the sentence, "And as time has gone by, that has strongly remained, until the spark of the Divine initiated that evolutionary separation to begin its course of turning back into Union." These great Divine Beings mentioned 2,600 years ago as a time when they began to "cultivate the gardens," and here they tell us more about the meaning of that phrase.

The human collective consciousness on Earth went through a process of separation that began about 14,000 years ago, which we will discuss further in Chapter Four. In December 2012, we ended a 26,000 year cycle. We are now entering a different process and a new age, in which we will find and acknowledge our Oneness, our Unity.

When the Holy Spirit is speaking in this book, a higher aspect of you and me is also speaking—we all are speaking at that moment, because we are all One.

The Divine Mother knows that we are all part of Her, and that all is One. She knows that it is part of Her and our Divine plan for this Earth that we would be separated from Her in our Earthly consciousness for a while, and then find our way back to Her.

When I said to Her that speaking with Her was like

finding our Mother whom we had not seen in a very long time, She replied, "And so it is." Notice how things are changing; you will find signs of a world already redefining itself. This Earth has already ascended to a higher consciousness, and She is patiently waiting for us to meet Her in an even higher consciousness, the consciousness of Oneness.

The session continues:

Malachi: *In this evolution of consciousness now, we honor greatly the evolution of Union. Humanity will come to [this] truth, and your religions must change. They cannot constantly stand in this endeavor of living and say that Mary is not Holy Spirit. They cannot stand in this endeavoring of truth and not allow it to be brought forward and spoken.*

And so you will keep your eyes open, will you not, to watch how this unfolds? That there will be the greater honoring of Mary, the Virgin Spirit, yes, purer Spirit—an ability to birth child without man. Yes, indeed, for She birthed all, did She not?

My wife and I have been speaking with Malachi for more than two years, and can say that he hardly says anything as bold as this. I feel that this is actually a message to the churches, that they must speak the truth about Mary and openly accept that She is the Holy Spirit and Mother God, the Divine Feminine, and the Great Birther. She is indeed a Virgin in spirit, as Malachi says, because She births all existence without need for man.

The churches will have to also recognize the natural human intercourse and conception that occurred between Mary and Joseph, in order to give birth to our most beloved Brother Jesus, Yeshua.

Malachi and the Divine Ones do not usually speak this way. They usually allow things to unfold in their own natural way in this world of Earth, which is a free will zone. But they are saying here that most of humanity will be able to discern truth in the near future, and that the sooner the churches reveal the truth, the better they will be received by the masses, and the more relevant their message will be.

If I may speak for our emerging humanity for a moment, I would love to be among the first to approach the leaders of the churches who openly agree to these truths and tell them that we love them, that all is forgiven, and now let's love our beautiful Divine Mother, the Holy Spirit. Let's recognize together that all people and all in existence in this world are Her children. We are all brothers and sisters of humanity.

Please realize that it is humanity's fears and doubts that have created the leaders who have spun misinformation for centuries, and that that situation has been self-fulfilling. Every focused thought that is not of Oneness is met by an opposing reality, which creates another opportunity for humankind to experience life without trust in the Oneness of the Holy Spirit.

Many people attract one abusive relationship after another, then blame the men or the women involved, or relationships in general. In fact, it is our own fears and doubts, our own expectations of being abused, that keep us repeatedly locked into creating the same environment.

Until we inwardly embrace the qualities that attract good into our lives, such as the qualities of Peace, self-love and appreciation, we will continue to be subject to karma's workshop. Once we are able to embrace Peace, appreciation, forgiveness, Unconditional Love and self-love, and respect without judgment, which are all forms of trust in the Holy Spirit, then we are no longer subject to the whims of karma.

Karma is a tool of the Divine plan for this planet, used by the soul. When we overcome karma, we take back our inalienable right and power to create our lives with joy and abundance.

The session continues:

Malachi: *But the choice to enter into the human form, for which indeed this gracious Holy Spirit created, was to honor it. And honor the mechanisms of the body created for the sperm and the egg to come together. In the vibrational intention, it was to bring that moment of conception into a purified state of being.*

What does that mean? It means that in this quality called the human body—both that one that was named Mary and that one named Joseph—that their minds, their emotions, their ego center, must indeed be in the purity of alignment. Meaning, they knew full well the state of their being, their Divine essence.

And in so doing, in that beautiful act of intercourse, it mattered not if they were married under [the] laws of humanity. It only mattered that they were unifying two bodies to bring forth a purer consciousness, so that humanity could be guided by a great teacher—their child, named Jesus. [Chuckles softly]

Why? So humanity could know [that] in body, one is the Holy Spirit. In body, one is the child of the Holy Spirit. In body, one can perform life as the Holy Spirit. Does this help you?

Kevin: Yes, thank you.

As you attempt to wrap your mind around all of this, keep in mind the concept of the Three in One. This is the original idea behind the Holy Trinity, which now can be stated as: the Holy Spirit, who is the Divine Mother, the Father, and the Son.

All of us are all three of these at the same time. We are the Divine Mother, because the Holy Spirit encompasses all existence, and as part of the Holy Spirit, we are also able to create and manifest. We are the Father, because we are Spirit in Action. And we are the Son, because we are also part of creation.

The beautiful essence of all existence, the Holy Spirit, has been speaking directly to us for a very long time. In Proverbs, She speaks to us as "I, wisdom." It is interesting that wisdom is referred to in the Bible as She, because it was once well known that the Holy Spirit is the Grand Wisdom of all existence.

Within the purity of wisdom, there is also ultimate truth and integrity. Find yourself in alignment with truth and integrity, and you will find yourself aligned with the Oneness of all, the Holy Spirit. As we are Her Truth, we become the example of Her Integrity here on Earth.

Some have thought that Wisdom is the Christ. But Wisdom, the Holy Spirit, existed before Christ. The Mother existed before the Son.

The Lord is the Grand or High Consciousness, and thus Jesus the Christ is a great part of the Grand Consciousness that we call "Lord." Just as Jesus is the Son of the Divine Mother, we are all Children of the Divine Mother and Divine Father.

Jesus came to us to set the example of a Christed Being, a Being who is God in body. We are also God in body, but almost none of us carry the awareness of this. Though some people may intellectually understand this, they may still not exemplify the pure states of Peace, Integrity and Truth.

These qualities are of the Holy Spirit; they bring Her Wisdom and Love into our waking consciousness and heart. More than just intellectualizing the knowledge that we are Holy Spirit, we need to live it with our actions, thoughts, heart and soul.

Jesus the Man did possess the Holy Spirit in its ultimate form, just as Father God possessed the Holy Spirit when They created the world. The Divine Masculine is the active component of the Holy Spirit. Possessing the Holy Spirit and Wisdom is not limited to women just because those things are of the Divine Feminine, and Divine Creation is not limited to men just because the act of creation is of the Divine Masculine. We all carry both attributes. Our very hearts beat by the life force of the Holy Spirit, and without it, life cannot exist.

Note that I often use the plural when describing the Divine Father, because we are all components of the Holy Spirit.

The Holy Spirit chose one of Her active components to be the representative of the Divine Father, and that was our beloved Saint Joseph. In the Grand World of Heaven, Saint Joseph is known as Saint Germain. Jesus and Saint Germain both achieved Christed mastery a very long time ago, after which both of them blended back into the Oneness of Spirit. Essentially, when one is blended with Holy Spirit, there is no need to manifest into life for the purpose of learning that we are all One, that we are all expressions of the Holy Spirit.

Malachi has told Marina and me when both Saint Germain and Jesus the Christ blended back to the Holy Spirit, they then received the call of service. They re-emerged into the Angelic realms and then into the material realms. This is why Holy Spirit chose Saint Germain and Jesus to be members of the Holy Family.

The Holy Family is symbolic of the beginning, when only the Holy Spirit existed. "I was created in the very beginning, even before the world began." (Proverbs 8:23) From our human point of view, we could say that the Holy

Spirit wanted friendship, interaction, and exploration of Her greatest qualities.

Keep in mind and in heart that all of us are in blended oneness with Holy Spirit, which is our original and eternal state of being.

How can we be there eternally, if we are here now? In the Grand World, there is no time, only levels of consciousness. The notion of linear time is a major characteristic of the third-dimensional Earth.

We each exist as Holy Spirit, as an Angel, and as a human, a component of Spirit living in matter. When we are living the life of an enlightened Christed being, then our consciousness actively includes the realization that we are components of Spirit.

At that point, the lower ego no longer operates our consciousness. We are then living in a higher state of consciousness called our Higher Self, which is second only to our Divine Self.

From Session L81 08.01.13:

Kevin: This question is for the Holy Spirit: In Proverbs, it says, "I, wisdom, was with the Lord when He began His work long before He had made anything else, as I was created before the very beginning, even before the world began."

I look at this as saying, "I am the Holy Spirit, Wisdom, and

I existed before the Father. Then I was with the Father, the Creator, before this World and all were created."

Malachi: *Indeed, indeed. You know by the passage [that] wisdom is Holy Spirit. You are correct.*

Here is the full text, from Proverbs 8:22-31 [New Century Version]:

> 22 "I, wisdom, was with the LORD when he began his
> work, long before he made anything else.
> 23 I was created in the very beginning,
> even before the world began.
> 24 I was born before there were oceans,
> or springs overflowing with water,
> 25 before the hills were there,
> before the mountains were put in place.
> 26 God had not made the earth or fields,
> not even the first dust of the earth.
> 27 I was there when God put the skies in place,
> when he stretched the horizon over the oceans,
> 28 when he made the clouds above
> and put the deep underground springs in place.
> 29 I was there when he ordered the sea not to go
> beyond the borders he had set. I was there when
> he laid the earth's foundation.
> 30 I was like a child by his side. I was delighted every day,
> enjoying his presence all the time,
> 31 enjoying the whole world,
> and delighted with all its people.

With the new understanding that there was once only the Holy Spirit in existence, we can understand why in Proverbs the Divine Mother says that She was like a child, innocent to the active side, the masculine side of Her being. She remains innocent to this day, viewing all as a child, in astonished wonder.

She loves all of Her children and is delighted with them, even those who have not led lives of Peace.

This is because She sees us as Herself, as the Divine. She knows the difficult course we have enrolled ourselves in. She offers us the food of Her wisdom while we are here on Earth, and eternal life in the higher dimensions once we have graduated from this human course.

I have wondered if we will all eventually be graced with eternal life, regardless of what beliefs we hold while in our Earth lives. I haven't asked the Divine this question yet, or heard them mention it in our sessions. They have said that they love every soul and are patient with every soul, even when it chooses to continue in a world of duality and violence after this world has ascended and achieved Heaven on Earth, as it is now in the process of doing. They have said they will create new worlds for these souls to continue their chosen experiences.

Based on the information that the beautiful Divine Beings have shared with me, I assume that we will all eventually blend into the Oneness of the Holy Spirit.

Here is the text from Proverbs 9:1-9 [New Century Version], on wisdom or foolishness:

> 1 Wisdom has built her house;
> she has made its seven columns.
> 2 She has prepared her food and wine;
> she has set her table.
> 3 She has sent out her servant girls, and she calls
> out from the highest place in the city.
> 4 She says to those who are uneducated,
> "Come in here, you foolish people!

5 Come and eat my food and drink
the wine I have prepared.
6 Stop your foolish ways, and you will
live, take the road of understanding.
7 "If you correct someone who makes fun of
wisdom, you will be insulted. If you correct
an evil person, you will get hurt.
8 Do not correct those who make fun
of wisdom, or they will hate you. But
correct the wise, and they will love you.
9 Teach the wise, and they will become
even wiser; teach good people, and
they will learn even more.

The Holy Spirit is saying here that this world of matter is a "free will" zone. Every person, every soul operating here on Earth has been given free choice. This choice must be respected, and the chosen path of the soul's evolution recognized, and not interfered with.

If a soul has chosen pain and suffering as its ultimate teacher, then how can one correct it? This is why some people are healed from energy healing sessions and some are not. Every healer must also first ask permission from the soul before offering the healing. The soul can then accept or refuse.

It's interesting that everything in this universe is negotiable; the healer can attempt to negotiate with the soul, to find a resolution that might lead the soul to choose a new path of learning that includes accepting a healing. You can negotiate with the soul, which is designing the curriculum of life for the evolution we experience here on Earth. But you can't step into the classroom and correct or judge the student. The classroom is this Earth, and the student is the human taking the courses of life set forth by the soul.

Considering all that, we might wonder, can the wise be corrected? The soul of the wise has already graduated its human self beyond the point at which pain, suffering and violence are the featured teachers of life.

These are students of a higher level. They have reached that level because they have asked the Divine many questions about spiritual life and growth, and don't mind being challenged about their own beliefs. They are not rigid in their thinking, so we can correct or question them, as long as we do it from the place where we are also not rigid in our beliefs.

The "good people" Wisdom refers to know that this world is not bigger or more important than the Holy Spirit and the Kingdom of God. These people have surrendered to the flow of Love, Peace and Wisdom that the Holy Spirit offers. Their faith and trust cannot be shaken off its foundation by mere words.

"Wisdom begins with respect for the LORD, and understanding begins with knowing the Holy One."

Malachi has said that "the Lord" is higher consciousness, which everyone has access to within themselves. When we respect the higher consciousness that is within us, we are cultivating its grand intelligence and releasing its mysteries. The true depth of all understanding stems from knowing that we are all of one Spirit, and that Spirit is the Holy Spirit, the Holy One. We are all holy expressions, both on this Earth and in Heaven.

"If you live wisely, you will live a long time; wisdom will add years to your life. The wise person is rewarded by wisdom, but whoever makes fun of wisdom will suffer for it."

This is similar to Jesus telling us not to judge or we will be judged, not to condemn or we will be condemned. The wise are also humble, and not rigid. The wise ask questions with an open mind and an open heart. The wise choose to spend some or most of their time finding the answers to the questions that life itself poses for us.

"Respect for the Lord" is also respect for obtaining higher consciousness. "Understanding the Holy One" is understanding the speaker here, for She is the Holy Spirit. The great understanding is to know that you are Divine, and part of the Holy Spirit. When we do not attempt to rise in consciousness and find our unity with Divinity, then we are subject to the Divine Laws of cause and effect, and subject to the consciousness of our soul.

The soul carries the commitment to inspire its human aspect to follow the enlightened path, to rise in consciousness and to grasp the truth of its unity with the Holy Spirit. When a person does not listen to their soul's guidance, then there is suffering.

It is said that, "When the going gets tough, the tough get going." Perhaps the tough are not always the wisest in that case, because when one is wise—resonating with peace, truth and integrity—things don't get as tough. That is one of the rewards of knowing Wisdom, the Holy Spirit.

Chapter Four

A History of Misinformation

Are your two-thirds of humanity ready to allow the Light? May we tell you, [that] you are very much there.

~ Malachi

In the last chapter Malachi was talking about the misinformation we've received about our spirituality, about Jesus, and of course about the Holy Mother, who has long been called the Virgin Mary by the Church.

You may be wondering why the Ascended Masters also refer to Mary this way, since Mary and Joseph have revealed to us that they conceived Jesus in the natural, Earthly way.

The Virgin Mother

In our Earth terms, "virgin" refers to someone who has never had sexual relations. In the Grand World of Heaven, and in the terms used by angels, Ascended Masters, and Holy

Spirit, the concept of the Virgin Mary refers to Mary's Divine Creator status. She is the virgin who has birthed All That Is, without need for a male—the seeding that takes place in conception. The Holy Spirit is the Holy Mother our Creator. She is the Great Birther of all of us and of all that exists.

The misinformation given us about "the Virgin" as She is spoken of here on Earth, was given to hide the fact that Mary and Joseph have both told us that there was intercourse in the conceiving of Jesus. Joseph was the biological father of Jesus, and Mary of course, was His biological mother.

She conceived the baby Jesus with Joseph, not via "the overshadowing of the Holy Spirit" as the Church has claimed, as if the Holy Spirit were something separate from who She is. They conceived Jesus in body and spirit, in the natural Earthly way, and had many other children in the same way.

The Holy Mother did not come here and incarnate upon the Earth in order to create a Great Being who would be unreachable to us. She came to birth a being who would be an example for us of someone who was able to achieve Christ consciousness while living an Earth life. That is why she chose to become human and to have a human baby.

Does she have the power of immaculate conception? Yes, of course she does. She could have created a child without the help of a biological father. But she chose to do everything in human terms, within the physics of humanity, so that she could birth someone fully human. A man who, like you and me, was birthed by a human mother and father. Someone who was made of flesh and bones, could feel pain, hunger and exhaustion, like you and me. Who had a need to love, to touch, and to have a family of His own, as all of us do.

She came to birth the example of a human being realizing their Divinity. She came to birth Jesus, to show us that we can be both Christed and fully human. To not feel guilty when we have made love to another person, but to rejoice in it. To rejoice that we've found union with another, and that the Divine also exists in the love we share with another.

Mary came to show us that we can practice creation, the same kind of creation that She practiced with another person. We're to fully live out our humanity, to make love with integrity, to be true to our partner if we have one, and to be true to ourselves.

Marriage was not created by the Holy Spirit, by Jesus the Christ, or by any Angelic being. Marriage is a human creation. But integrity is a virtue, extremely respected in what we will call the Angelic Realm.

Letting Go of Separateness

Let's not continue to create institutions of marriage, of religion, or of government. Our institutions have drawn lines around the planet, creating separations between people, nations, religions and ethnicities. Think of the largest puzzle imaginable, with a vast number of small pieces—this is what our institutions have done.

We have so many religions, so many sects that are constantly dividing, then dividing further. Buddhism and Christianity alone have created thousands of sects and denominations. Hinduism and Islam have also drawn many lines between and among themselves. Most religions create divisions, instead of creating unity, which is the ultimate goal for humans on this planet Earth.

What matters to the Angels, to Jesus, and to the Holy Spirit, is only one goal: for everyone to find and be aware of the Oneness of all.

Anything that separates people, any living beings who are not in alignment with the goal of unity, are not in alignment with Spirit. For when someone comes to the awareness of Oneness, to the awareness that they are truly part of and one with the Holy Spirit, then their awareness evolves into what is called the Christed awareness or Christ consciousness.

Attaining the Christ Consciousness

To become Christed, we must have not only an intellectual understanding of the awareness that we are all One, that we are all Holy Spirit. We must also embody that idea, living it in our actions, thoughts and emotions. Then we will radiate the Christ consciousness as we interact with others and our environment, as well as in our prayers, thoughts and meditations.

In the light of this possibility, which is there for everyone, we can see that the Holy Mother's incarnation upon this beautiful Earth was the greatest gift She could have given us. Because within that Earth life, the Holy Mother gave us the gift of the Person of the Christ, Jesus.

Activation of the Pineal Gland, the Third Eye

Much of Jesus' Christed consciousness was based on the fact that He was born with a fully activated pineal gland.

The pineal gland, named for its pine cone shape, is located well behind the center of the forehead. It works in connection with the pituitary gland and the medulla.

Scientists say we only utilize 5 to 15 percent of our brain. The unused sectors of the brain work in conjunction with the 95 percent of our DNA that has been called "junk DNA," because it appears to have no biological function. Malachi tells us however, that all of our DNA has great function, and the ability to spark the growth of those parts of our brain that will soon be taking on higher Light frequencies.

At present, the "junk DNA" has not yet been decoded by science. But it was created to work with the pineal gland to aid in our ascension into Light beings of higher consciousness.

Currently, human beings operate on only two strands of DNA, though part of the development we will experience in this new era entails regaining use of all twelve of our original DNA strands.

The pineal gland acts as the master station of the

DNA. It works as a control center, sending messages to the pituitary gland and the medulla, the part of the brainstem that controls automatic behaviors such as breathing. Where the pituitary gland regulates reason and logical thought, the pineal gland regulates feeling, intuition and symbolic thought.

A fully activated pineal gland—one not calcified by fluoride and a poor diet—renders us capable of the great intuitive and even psychic ability that Christ had. Called the third eye, it is connected to the sixth chakra, which receives premonitions and spiritual insight, as well as being a doorway to higher consciousness.

With this gland and all DNA strands fully activated, we will have many of the abilities that Christ had. It is part of the potential within every human being. The first secret to activating that potential is to acquire the consciousness of Peace, and to remain at Peace regardless of what is happening in our outer lives.

Each of us has the ability to be a Christ, though that potential is not yet activated. Many are on their way to opening and activating their third and fourth strands of DNA, and their pineal gland.

It is not at all a coincidence that the current reactivation of the fourth strand of human DNA is coinciding with the Earth entering the fourth dimension in our current era.

Hidden History

Let's return to the spread of misinformation about

the Holy Mother's true identity. This covering up was intentional, to hide the fact of a Divine Mother who is also the Holy Spirit.

It was not always this way. There was once a Golden Age of awareness, a time when both Atlantis and Lemuria still existed as thriving continents. Lemuria was a very large continent in the Pacific Ocean. All that remains of it now are a few islands. Atlantis was a continent in the Atlantic Ocean, and likewise only exists now as a few islands and underwater pyramids in the area of the Bahamas and Bermuda. The islands are the Atlantean mountain peaks and high elevation land that survived the destruction of the continent.

The Golden Age ended with the fall of Atlantis more than 14,000 years ago. The Dark Age followed, which is the age that we were born into.

Since the beginning of the Dark Age thousands of years ago, Earth has been ruled by a self-serving, powerful elite, who have little or no conscience regarding how they treat our Earth or Her people. Many of the people who are among the "dark side" have a different lineage than most of us, and their families require them to maintain their exclusive bloodlines. They contain a higher percentage of bloodlines that are sometimes considered to be royal lineage.

We won't focus on the details of the dark side—who they are, where they came from, and how they have maintained their political and economic power through the centuries, though that power is now slipping away from them. It's important that we carry certain facts to our awareness, without becoming prey to a reaction of anger, fear or helplessness.

Those negative human emotions are not in alignment with Truth, and only exist in the human mind, the lower ego mind, which can also be called the reptilian brain. The lower ego is the mind that says, in fearful terms, "Me, me, me! What can I do to get what I want to get? How can I survive? How can I conquer?" It is the thing we are here to overcome.

The Golden Age

The Golden Age was a world of beautiful temples made of crystal, of many priests and priestesses who devoted their time and efforts to achieving the highest possible spiritual connection with the higher realms. It was a time of free energy, where great crystals were grown under mountains, in places such as the area that is now Arkansas.

Underground tunnels from this time still exist today. They once linked Atlantis to the Arkansas area and other parts of the world. These great crystals worked in conjunction with what we'll call a second moon, which acted like a satellite, beaming out the loving energies of people on Earth.

The crystals also received energy from the second moon. This was a pure, harmless energy that was free for everyone to use. This is why no combustion engines or similar technology have been found in archaeological digs that have discovered artifacts from this era. However, there have been vehicles found that were made to float or hover, and other vehicles that simply needed some type of receptor to operate as an antigravity device.

Antigravity devices were also used to move huge monolithic stones. During the Golden Age, structures such as Stonehenge and the pyramids were built with far greater ease than we can even imagine. The ancient ones achieved this by using sound vibration to nullify the gravity of an object. Monolithic stones could therefore be precisely placed in exact positions, with very little effort.

Building materials used in this era included stone and cement. The cement they created was much more advanced than what we use today, and used all natural materials, such as eggs.

In his excellent book *Fingerprints of the Gods: The Evidence of Earth's Lost Civilization*, author Graham Hancock explains that when modern archaeologists broke open a monolithic stone block from the pyramids in Egypt, they found human hair inside of it. Though the technology of this Golden Age far surpassed our own, it was achieved in unison with Mother Nature.

Interestingly, as Earth ascends to higher dimensions, we will see many of our technologies become obsolete. Why would we need a cell phone, for example, when we're able to speak with someone telepathically? Why would we need airplanes, when we can travel within the energy of the shimmering light?

Precession

The Golden Age ended due to a great astrological cycle of precession that moved us from the Age of Leo into the Age of Cancer. This was the era in which Earth pulled away from its geographical alignment with the River of Light, the stream of Divine particles that some have called the Photon Belt, which rained down upon and blessed the Earth with higher Light frequencies for so many thousands of years.

In astronomy, "precession" refers to any of several slow changes in an astronomical body's rotational or orbital limits, and especially to the Earth's precession of the equinoxes. The equinoxes move in a westerly direction, unlike the Sun, which moves east along its ecliptic—the path that it travels amongst the stars.

It is called a precession because the ages are actually moving backwards in relationship to the Earth. That is why we have just entered the Age of Aquarius, after leaving the Age of Pisces.

An age lasts about 2,160 years and an eon lasts about 26,000 years. As we come into the Age of Aquarius, we also enter into a new eon, toward a new placement upon the wheel of precession.

The Manipulation of Humankind

When Earth was still on the cusp between the Ages of Leo and Cancer, people began falling prey to the negative influence and manipulation of the "dark ones." (This term does not describe their appearance, only the shadowy density of their consciousness.) These were beings whose bloodlines contained the very dark energy of a people who had come to Earth intentionally seeking a third-dimensional world they could conquer and control.

During that cusp period, people were easily brainwashed, tempted and manipulated into violence and despair. The dark ones were spinning their webs, laying traps and spreading misinformation throughout the world. At the same time, they created reasons to immerse people in the feelings that create separation, feelings that did not flow with the image of the Divine. Feelings of fear, greed, anger and vengeance.

The Reptilian Brain

One of the tactics the dark ones used often was to start wars. They constantly created a feeling of urgency and fear, similar to our current political system, which creates fear with reports of what we call "terrorism." By constantly repeating the words "terrorism" and "terror, terror, terror" they are able to embed feelings and images of fear into people's minds.

These specifically embed themselves into the reptilian brain, hyper-activating it. This is the part of the brain that seeks only to survive, and to serve itself. That part of the brain is capable of deciding, "I will do anything to survive, even kill. Even if I have to look at another people, country, race or religion and say, 'Kill them all.'" The reptilian brain thinks this way, because it wants to survive by any means.

That level of consciousness is the basis of the service-to-self philosophy of the dark ones.

The lower ego, the engineer of the reptilian brain, is our holographic mind. This is the mind that thinks that outer reality is the only reality that exists. It is the part of the mind that usually controls us in this game we call life on Earth. It is the mind that we need to re-train in order to become enlightened, to be Christed and rise to the level of Christ consciousness.

There is also a higher ego, which is connected to the higher self, which is the true spirit of who we are. This higher self lives at one with the Holy Spirit. When we come from a place of higher vibration such as Love and Peace, we are operating from the higher mind, or higher self.

The New Age

We have just completed the eon that started close to 26,000 years ago, and have entered the Age of Aquarius. We are still on the cusp of that age, which means that the Age of Pisces still carries some influence.

As of 2013, we have entered both a new age and a new eon. This is undoubtedly where the New Age movement got its name. These are people who perceived the coming of the Age of Aquarius as having the characteristics so wonderfully depicted in the song, "Aquarius/Let the Sunshine In" from the musical *Hair.* The lyrics of that song perfectly point to what we look forward to seeing in a fifth-dimensional Earth—written and performed by a band called The 5th Dimension:

"Harmony and understanding. Sympathy and trust abounding/No more falsehoods or derisions, golden living, dreams of visions/Mystic crystal revelation, and the mind's true liberation/Aquarius, Aquarius."[1]

It is difficult to think of the people of the Golden Age, who clearly had this greater awareness, being brought down by fear, temptation, manipulation, misinformation and greed. But once human consciousness descended into the lower ego, people were easily manipulated and controlled, especially by fear.

Though the dark ones were hard at work to achieve human regression, let us remember that there are no humans or spirits in existence who are not of the Light, in the final sense. No beings exist who are not of Source, of the Holy Spirit. These beings we call the dark ones intentionally separated themselves from that awareness, and grouped together to form alliances whose agendas were to control others, so that they would never be controlled themselves. Their goal was to gain power over the masses, to control the belief systems of the masses, and to gain and maintain power indefinitely.

Fear as Manipulation

These beings knew about the 666 gateway. They knew that two-thirds of mass consciousness broke down to .666, and that is what is needed in the thought process, in the belief systems of the masses, to take control over what is created on this planet. The dark ones of Atlantis knew this, and over many years, were able to sway two-thirds of Atlantean humanity into the misguided emotions of fear and doubt over those of Faith, Peace and Love.

Urgency arose, as they then wanted to use the advanced technology of these great crystals, this great energy, for military purposes. They talked many people into this terrible misuse. They probably used propaganda statements such as, "Save your life. . . We have to win the war, or you and your family will be killed. You're going to be controlled. . . you're going to be conquered. We must attack and we must kill. . . kill them all if possible, to rid ourselves of this enemy."

But the only enemy was the consciousness they had put forth. So the remaining leaders of the Golden Age, some of them known as Atla-Ra, took as many of these crystals and technology as they could through the underground tunnels, carrying them to safe places around the world, mostly within the quadrant of the Americas.

Also at this time, the consciousness of the second moon made a decision, along with the consciousness of the All, the Holy Spirit, that it must leave. And so it made its way to what was perhaps its original birthplace, the star system of Arcturius.

The Beginning of the Age of Misinformation

It was at this time that the system of misinformation began, sometime between 13,000 and 14,000 years ago. So much misinformation was created, that the very birthplace of that misinformation is said to not even exist. Whole continents that once existed have since been said to have never existed except in myths and fairy tales. We all know about the deluge that happened just after this time. I have not asked about that yet in our sessions with the Ascended Masters, but perhaps it was the Holy Spirit's way of trying to cleanse the Earth of those who had taken it over.

This is how we come to have the story of Noah. As Graham Hancock states in *Fingerprints of the Gods*, there are close to one hundred different versions of the "Noah and the Flood" story that are told around the world, each telling how their own race and civilization survived the great flood and storms. Whether it was by finding refuge on high ground, deep in caves, or in boats, a portion of the human race did survive, but it was a very small percentage compared to the number that had existed during the Golden Age.

From Session L35 on 8.24.11:

Malachi speaks here about the second moon:

Malachi: *It was called Junier. You say, did they fly it out somewhere? No, beautiful one, they did not. It did move out, on [to] a different orbiting system. Do you know why?*

Kevin: Why?

Malachi: *Because of the negativity that was taking form on the*

Earth plane consciousness. It is a vibration that was used, yes, to harness universal energies. It was [originally there to broadcast] a vibration of positivity and of great creativity, and with that, beautiful one, when the misuse became too much, you may say [that] the Great Creator took that moon out of its orbit.

Where did it go? Well, it moved into the Gateway of Arcturus. It has been making its way back towards your Earth plane, beautiful one, for approximately twenty of your years.

It has already sent much of the vibrations back into consciousness, into human beings that are searching for the higher wisdom. And you yourself, beautiful one, shall you wish to tap into its vibration, its encouragement, and its vibrational insights?

When you meditate, go to the back of your head. Go to the ancient memory point, which is called your medulla, do you understand that? Then, beautiful one, you will begin to feel the contact of Junier, and that contact will give you impressions in the mind, sensations in your feeling tone, and wisdom thoughts that come to you.

The evolution of your mankind is presently in its great destructive field, and that is good. That is not bad, it is good. Do you understand?

Kevin: Not really, no.

Malachi: *Well, then we'll do it again. It is part of the evolution of the transmutation, meaning you're readying yourselves to enter into the vibration of a new evolution, and you call it a New World. Do you understand that?*

Kevin: Yes.

Malachi: *To do this, to allow the Junier to come forward, we have been asking all of you human beings to let go of the memories that you carry now. The belief structures that you carry now. So you can get to the purest form of energy once again. So it's called destruction, meaning letting go. Releasing and allowing the new to emerge.*

Now let's do that in this form: Beautiful one, let's have you think of a seed that's placed in a ground. When that seed begins to burst it must destruct what is encompassing it, must it not?

Well, think of that for yourselves. You're a seed in the ground, have been a seed in the ground, and that of yourselves are bursting forth. You're sprouting. Do you understand?

But that which has encased you is now destroying itself, so that the beautiful strength of you can come forward. And if you watch the plant sprout itself up through the soil, there has to be a destruction in the moment of the soil, to let it pass through, is there not?

And when it comes again to grow further, its stem must allow a breakthrough. Therefore, that is called a destruction, to allow that of other frequencies, of leaves and flowers and fruits to occur. Must it not?

Kevin: Yes.

Malachi: *Every time, a destructive force. Now, you of the human race kind, and even the galaxy that you're within, has been undergoing these stations of destructions. And you are ready to finish off that [which] has been, so that you may come into the new beginning of the Peaceful Lights, of the radiant Light bodies you pray for and desire to know.*

Now, as Junier comes forward again, notice that that is from the greatest Creator. It is not humanity. It is not that which you called extra-terrestrial beings that are switching it off or switching it on. You switch it off or switch it on, by attitudes, by harmonies or disharmonies. In other words, you create a veil, and you cannot see it.

Now, as you allow yourselves to come more into your internal harmony, to let go of that which you have known, and to allow yourself, as we have said, feel the energies at the back of your head. The most ancient of ancient of Holy of Holy knowledge resides there. What also resides there is the All-Seeing Eye. As you allow yourselves to open up to the truer mystery, to the truer memory, you will allow that vibration to also trigger your pineal gland, that which is termed the philosopher's stone, the all-wise one.

And that takes what? It takes the practice of your thoughts, the practice of your meditations, and the practice of your union with the one Great Spirit.

Now, beautiful one, while we are talking to you, you are having [a] movement of consciousness that is allowing you to touch base with all of that, are you not?

As Malachi was speaking, I was doing what he was suggesting and focusing upon my medulla. I was able to travel inwardly to the Gateway of Arcturus, then connect with the second moon, Junier. Malachi knew exactly what was going on in my mind. There have been quite a few times when Malachi, Jesus, Saint Germain and the Holy Mother have read my mind or commented on the activity of my mind.

Malachi: *And you know it has taken you only but a few moments, has it not?*

Kevin: Yes.

Malachi: *Now continue to blend and re-blend, to connect and re-connect, and to have a trusting within yourself. This vibration is going to emerge from within you, in such a fashion that it will begin to shape-shift your words out of your own mouth, your thoughts in your own brain's mind-thinking.*

They will be different, and at first will feel quite foreign. And as they form the words from the vibrations, the words will appear foreign for a time. You will have a field vision, meaning you are sensing the dimensions from which you are exploring the Junier presentation of energy. Do you understand?

Kevin: Yes.

Malachi: *Does that help you?*

Kevin: Yes.

Malachi: *Very good.*

Kevin: [to Marina] Do you feel it? How do you feel the vibration?

Malachi: [to Marina] *Beautiful one, I shall tell you how he felt it. He shall confirm. I shall tell you how you can feel it, and you will confirm. He allowed his mind to go to the back of his head and reach his medulla.*

Marina: Yes.

Malachi: *He allowed his energy then to expand from his body/mind conscious, from his brain/body consciousness, and he went what is called into and beyond Arcturus, and he connected with Junier and connected to Source. And he drew that energy back into [and] through that beautiful back side of his head. Do you understand?*

Marina: Yes.

Malachi: *Now take a breath. Be aware of the focus of your mind. Do you feel it at the front of your head?*

Marina: Yes.

Malachi: *Now let yourself track that energy to the back of your head, to the far back, and just above the neck, where you will connect with what is called the medulla.*

So if you let yourself, again, feel yourself into the galaxies. Feel yourself calling yourself into gateways of star patterns. We call you to Arcturus. It begins to take you right away from your own galaxy.

It allows you then to begin to feel what is called an ancient wisdom base, and that which has been called the second moon of Earth, Junier. You'll find the grace of the Divine there, for it was also a satellite, carrying all knowledge. Do you understand?

Marina: Yes.

Malachi: *It was a satellite, that when utilized by the human being accepting the radiance of the vibration, it not only travels back to what your bodies feel as the back of your head, the medulla, but it does indeed begin to vibrate the pineal gland, and even the pituitary gland of your human body.*

When you feel the pituitary gland in action, you'll also feel the channel above your head. You'll call it the seventh chakra. Did you feel that, beautiful one?

Kevin: Yes.

Malachi: *And so this is where you are allowing even more thoughts, more vibrations, higher resonance of energy frequencies, and they pass through you. And when they pass through you, they pass through the center core of you, called a Hara line, [a] light vibrating Source within you. Now what do you feel?*

Marina: I feel warm, mellow energy and something blue.

Malachi: *Very good. The something blue, beautiful one, is the Hara line you have activated. Very good, and you may meditate together, can you not? And bring that energy forward. What I am going to ask you both to do, is to have another sense of energy. You see, as you both have activated that vibration, do you realize how you immediately share it with your son? Can you feel that?*

Kevin and Marina: Yes.

Malachi: *Then know [that] you assist him.*

From Session L55 on 6.7.12 - The Two-Thirds or .666 Gateway

Malachi: *In the consciousness of every human being it takes two-thirds of their selves to align with one thought, one feeling to allow a manifestation to occur.*

In the vibration of the collective conscious, it is the same. If two-thirds of you are aligned in one thought, one emotion, one truth, you [collectively] manifest it. Do you understand?

You are asking these dark forces [to release] that [which] have been holding a grip on the consciousness for some time here on planet Earth. And are they ready to be released from that task? They are indeed. And are your two-thirds of humanity ready to allow the Light? May we tell you, [that] you are very much there.

Kevin: Oh, nice!

Malachi: *So do not fear when it looks the opposite. But also realize that there is still that pattern of the free will choice, and whenever those who appear, to their own frightfulness, to not have the same stance or the same condition of control that they had before, they become strong fighters, do they not? And so will they win out and call [the] two-thirds back over into their alignment?*

Kevin: No.

Malachi: *They cannot, as long as those of you who hold the Light, [are] holding sacred truth, non-judgment and Unconditional Love. For then there can be no fight—there is no fuel.*

So we will highly encourage you, yes. Be in the Light of the highest intention, with the positive knowing [that] now is the time for this shift. In the shift of the consciousness, that which has been held in the shadows and the darkness of the human force field, in the allowance that human beings did do, which was [to] allow anything to take over—that has been shifting strongly throughout your world.

The Flood

Let's return to the history of the great flood. During this deluge, the dark ones survived by flying away or staying underground. They had maintained the technology to fly in terms of craft similar to helicopters. Whether these used combustion or some other form of technology is not known, but they did manage to leave, then return after the disaster was over.

When they came back, they focused on three ancient lands: Mesopotamia, India and Egypt, to start new civilizations. By this time, Atlantis was no more. The oceans had risen about 400 feet higher than where they had been previously. This may have occurred due to the melting of massive icecaps around the planet. Parts of the Americas and the Great Lakes remained underwater at this time.

The "royal" bloodline families then separated, each to start a kingdom in one of these three separate lands. During this time, these civilizations were developed into the Eastern and Middle Eastern ancient cultures, as we know them. Mesopotamia and Egypt developed under the influence of what remained of Atlantean civilization. The Indian civilization developed mostly with the influence of what remained of Lemurian civilization, with Atlantean influence.

Then the aggressive misinformation campaigns and agendas went forward. The dark ones decided to simply erase the history of the Golden Age. As if human history had only been written on a blackboard, they took an eraser and erased everything prior to the point at which they had taken control.

His-Story

This was the start of what we know now is the new version of history, or his-story. It's what the dark ones gave us, a fiction that served their own purposes.

They've told us that the human race followed a linear path, evolving from apes that eventually stood up, then evolving into the Homo erectus, then the Homo sapiens.

They've told us that in our earliest times, humans only used rocks and spearheads as tools. Then fire was utilized, and eventually our brains developed enough to create more advanced human cultures.

You might be thinking, wouldn't we have found archeological evidence suggesting that this new history was fabricated?

Actually, we do have evidence. As archeologists dig, they find all different types of humans. Some are giants and some are as small as hobbits. There were many different types of humans, not just Neanderthals. And we also find that the evolution of humanity was not always linear. These ideas were kept from us, because they don't jibe with the beliefs that the dark ones concocted.

The dark ones created these new civilizations. Some scholars call Sumeria, or Sumer, of Mesopotamia, the cradle of civilization. In truth, it was the rebirth of human civilization, as were Egypt and India.

The misinformation continued forward. Gods were created in the names of the dark ones. The Greek gods, the Egyptian gods. Who are they? They are the dark ones—humans, almost just like us, who had the technology to take on the characteristics of gods.

The Ancient Bloodlines

The dark ones were not quite like us, because many of them were and still are humans who maintained what became known as royal lineage. These are the bloodlines of a particular people who have a different lineage then most human beings, though it is not a "higher" or better lineage, as they would have us think.

Those royal bloodlines still exist, though many are kept in secret. Many of these families have continued to rule in the areas of banking, religion, government and the military, for centuries. In fact, many of the presidents of the United States can be traced back to the bloodline or family lineage of Ramses, the Pharaoh of Egypt. Note the images of pyramids on the U.S. currency. Many U.S. presidents have also been tied in with the bloodlines of British royalty and Winston Churchill.

Several centuries ago, two sisters from these bloodline families came to the United States, and went on to create two powerful families in U.S. politics and finance. One branch is now the powerful Bush family, from which many politicians, including two presidents, have sprung. The other branch is the powerful Forbes family, whose members include former U.S. senator, presidential nominee and Secretary of State John Kerry.

The Free Will Zone

It's important to remember, when we see the modern day implications of what the dark ones created, that this information is not meant to lead to pointing fingers, directing anger, starting wars or creating violence. Because when we do that, we are operating on the level of the dark ones. We are inadvertently aiding their cause.

It doesn't matter if it's in the name of God, the name of Holy Spirit, the name of justice, the name of Christ, or the name of Abraham. Any act of violence, any prejudice or bitterness held against another, is not in alignment with God, Holy Spirit, the Ascended Masters, the great Angels, the Archangels, and all the great cosmic beings. For their agenda is an agenda of Peace, and only in Peace will they act.

This Earth, this three-dimensional world we have been living in, is as we've said, a free will zone. In that free will zone, you were given that egoic lower mind—the reptilian brain, if you will, and the freedom to make your own choices. And even Mother and Father God will not overstep your free will choices.

That is the game here. I know that as we experience life, it seems very real and not at all holographic. We have many hardships and losses here, including the losses of loved ones, and I don't mean to diminish the nature of these hardships.

Waking Our Higher Consciousness

Yet this life on Earth is like a game. We come into this world with our higher consciousness asleep. Children are partially awakened when small, but usually by the age of seven, the higher consciousness goes to sleep for the most part, and their conscious self falls to their lower ego. Because the higher consciousness views the rest of the world in its duality, with its violence and anger, the higher consciousness, the higher ego, goes to sleep. It does this because that Divine part of us can only exist in peace, and in full Christed awareness.

As we forget who we are, that we are the true Angels of the Holy Spirit and the true Oneness of the Holy Spirit, we come into our Earth lives karmic-bound. Every experience, every relationship, every pain and suffering, every joy and success, every laugh and recognition of beauty, are all part of our ultimate lessons to find our true selves, and to move our focus from our lower ego to our higher ego, so as to know Holy Spirit.

This is what we call rebirthing, being reborn into the Holy Spirit. Yes, the realization and awareness of the Holy Spirit went to sleep in us for a while, but it is never fully asleep, in the totality. Reawakening the Holy Spirit is not something that can just be done in a rite or initiation, though that can put us on the path. We must seek the qualities of the Holy Spirit, seek to be Holy Spirit, to have that presence fully activated within us. That quality is best reached by maintaining Peace.

Maintaining Peace

We can be at Peace, no matter what is happening around us. No matter who is condemning, judging, threatening or hurting us or those we love.

Is that easily done? It definitely is not. Can it be done? Yes. Jesus set that example. Stories of Him screaming and yelling in anger or pain are not based in truth. When He is shown as being a Man of Peace, finding Peace in all situations, whether people are dying and suffering or attacking Him, that is the Man Jesus, and that can be all of us as well.

Through Jesus' words and instruction, my wife and I are learning how to stay in Peace, and we will share this information with everyone. It's not easy at first, but I have dramatically improved. I still get irritated, but only about 2 percent as often as I used to. I used to argue with my family, but no longer do so.

I feel no need for war. I sense love in every being. I love my country, but I also love every human being on Earth. Every single one of us is the Divine incarnated, a holy expression of the Divine, though most of us are asleep to that reality.

I've now devoted a great portion of my life, not to telling people what's right and what's wrong, or what's wrong with their thinking, but to writing, speaking and healing, with the goal of encouraging others to set out upon a new path. A path that will lead to recognition of our Oneness, that will erase not the truth, but the lines of separation that are webbed throughout humanity and its belief systems.

Two-Thirds of Humanity

I also seek to inspire others to enter a path that will bring the one-third still in darkness into the Light.

We know that when two-thirds of humanity embrace Oneness, embrace the Holy Spirit of Light and Love, then we will have Heaven on Earth. Then all those other belief systems, and all those pieces of misinformation, misguidance, fallacies, unwanted and unjust laws, will disappear soon after that.

Then the world will truly be a New World, in a New Age and a New Eon. Then the goals and agendas of the world will change. Then many people will say, "I don't want to just work for a living. I want to work for the good of humanity." Or perhaps volunteer, and help those who are still suffering, help those who are still hungry, who have gone through much trauma and pain.

There will be those who have such a strong desire to heal our beautiful Mother Earth, to clean and purify beautiful Mother Earth, to give Her love and devotion. And there will be those who will spread words and blessings of Light, who will be agents of Light—Lightworkers—and their numbers will continue growing exponentially.

Then we will get to a point when the Divine Ones will be seen. We will have more visual manifestations of the Angels, Ascended Masters, the Holy Spirit Mother God, and all the Divine Masculine incarnations of enlightened beings. Some of them will appear here on Earth, and we'll talk to them.

Why don't they appear here now? You may be asking. If they did so, while humankind is still in its current consciousness, it would be considered an oddity, an event. It would create a group of followers for those who saw and for those who believed. Then a separation would occur for those who didn't see and didn't believe. The Ascended Masters do not want followers, and they do not want any events and ideas happening that will create any more separation.

Becoming Inspired

We are here to be inspired, to follow our higher selves and the presence of the I Am, the presence of the Holy Spirit within us.

Just because the Holy Spirit incarnated as Mary, the mother of Jesus, doesn't mean we must all convert to Christianity. We only have to convert to the idea of Oneness, in any form that we find it. That path of enlightenment can be found through Buddha, through Allah, through Zoroaster, and through many other belief systems.

I once asked Jesus, "If someone is born in the Amazon jungle and has never heard of Jesus Christ, do they have an equal chance to find their Oneness? To be Christed?" His answer was a definite "Yes!"

Many religions that do not recognize Jesus as God still recognize Him as a Master, a great teacher and prophet. Paramahansa Yogananda wrote many positive and enlightening books about Jesus. He may have been one of the most prolific writers about Jesus within the last hundred years, though he was not a Christian in a narrowly defined sense.

A Growing Awareness of Truth

There are many truths now being brought to light after ages of misinformation. We discuss some of them in this book—the truth that Mary did have sexual relations with Joseph before they married, and that Jesus was conceived in the natural way. We've also learned what would have been unthinkable to earlier generations—that the Holy Spirit is not a He, but a She.

Humankind is also now gaining a greater awareness of what the Holy Spirit is. It is possible to feel and communicate with Her, depending on how you communicate inwardly. I'm a "feeler"; I can feel Her energy almost anytime. It may take a few minutes, but I will feel Her presence, Her energy, often in the palm of my hands.

Some people can speak to Mother God easily, as my wife Marina can. Many of you will also do these blessed things. Some may see flashes of light, or see or perceive Her in other ways. I did see Her, and Saint Germain as well, when I was a child. They would come to my bed at night and just watch over me. Though I don't see them now, I look forward to the day when I will see them again. I am extremely grateful that Marina and I can talk to them.

Playing Our Music

We all have different gifts and talents, which humanity has a great need for. All our gifts and talents combined create a great symphony. We all have our music to play, and all of it is needed. Play your music. When you feel inspired to do something in your life, you must follow that impulse, whatever it is.

You might want to plant and tend a beautiful garden.

Or you might be inspired to write poetry, compose music, or paint. Or maybe you're just going to live your life as a living example of Peace, happiness and joy, going to places where you can live out that life purpose to the highest benefit of humankind.

Perhaps you're here to embody higher frequencies of Light or healing. It may be your role to emanate those frequencies in different places in the world. Each of us comes to the Earth with natural gifts and abilities that we are meant to share in one way or another, whether grandly or quietly.

Others will not necessarily see or know how to draw out our gifts and potentials. It is up to each of us to discover them ourselves, to BE them and to live them out, to BE the holy expression of who we truly are.

Don't feel that you have to follow anything that was created, devised or written in the last eon of time, which ended in 2012. We are in a new age now, and many new roles, jobs, gifts and abilities will increasingly be discovered in the coming years. You may already be living out some of them.

New Paths for a New Age

The Mayan calendar actually ended on October 28, 2011. The eon ended sometime between then and December 2012. As of 2013, we are in a new eon. It is important now to fully begin this new time, to discover the wisdom of your higher self, and the wisdom found in the work of the many

Lightworkers who are now bringing out the truth around the world. Find out whose work you are naturally drawn to—not to be a follower of them, but to be inspired by them. Then when you've become inspired enough, create your own path.

Become the inspirer, a person of inspiration whose talents are woven throughout your being and are growing to maturity. Use your gifts, even as they are still growing.

Coming Out of the Ego

As you grow and share your gifts, don't allow the outward-rippling vibrations of others to reach you in a way that causes you to react from the ego, like a puppet whose strings have been pulled. When questioned or insulted about their work or viewpoint, most people would have a reaction. They might argue or trade insults, or want to cry out of frustration or hurt feelings.

We need to learn to not be reactive. Saint Germain has taught me to not react negatively to anything that is occurring around me. We should react to life. But we need to react in Peace, from the awareness of our basic Oneness. If you can do that, then the Angels will be with you.

When we react from our own lower ego, we are subject to the Divine laws of cause and effect. Reactive behavior is behavior that is caught in the web of the third dimension, of the matrix created by the dark ones. We don't need to be puppets anymore—not in terms of emotion, action, or believing misinformation.

The Third Member of the Trinity

The Bible states that Mary was a literal virgin at the time of Jesus' conception. It also states that the Holy Spirit is a He. But it is hard to believe that the Holy Trinity represents three males—Him, Him and Him. There is no balance there, unlike the male/female balance we find everywhere in the natural world. We already have two "men" in the trinity—a Father and a Son. The properties of the Divine Feminine are the Presence that lends perfect balance to creation, to the universe, and to our beliefs.

The Holy Spirit is the Divine Mother who created All, including the other members of the Holy Family. She incarnated here as Mary to demonstrate for us the truth of the identity of the Holy Spirit. Her secret was hidden by powerful forces, the self-appointed elite who are often referred to as the cabal, the Illuminati, or the Anunnaki.

Again, we will not focus on the details of the dark side. We will not blame, accuse or judge them, or seek to imprison or punish them. If we did that, we would only find ourselves dragged into the lower vibrations that we're seeking to climb out of, in this new eon.

Make your Peace with them, even after you hear of everything that they have done, for their days in power are running down quickly. They will not be allowed to remain with us here on Earth as we enter the fourth, then fifth dimensions, unless they embrace the Light and the qualities of the Divine Feminine, not only in their own private belief systems, but also in the greater doctrines they subscribe to.

The Importance of Sending Light and Love

We can all speed up the process of cleansing this Earth of all lower vibrations by sending this group Love, and shining Light upon them. We can speed the process of bringing this world into a state of Universal Peace by sending Love and Light to the areas where the dark webs are spun the tightest. Places of war, poverty and suffering.

Wherever in the world we find individuals given to lower impulses and lower vibrations, we can send them Light and Love. Just by raising our own consciousness and being committed to Peace and Love, we help to raise the overall vibration of the planet.

By committing to all that helps to create a realization of Oneness, we can all help to erase the lines of separation in this world. Whenever we make another—the eternal Them—into an enemy, even just in discussion, we've created another line of separation.

We can help to create the Oneness. We can trust in God, our Angels, our Ascended Masters, Holy Spirit, and in the Divine laws of this planet, that there is a course for those who choose to repel that Light. There is a path ready for those who continue to support the drastic dark/Light duality that has existed on this planet. Those who refuse to absorb the higher frequencies of Light and Love will eventually leave this planet. They will be reborn into another world, where they can continue their dualistic life in the third dimension. That is their soul choice and their soul's path, and it must be respected, just as the Angels and the Holy Spirit have respected our paths, when we came into this three-dimensional world of duality, possibly thousands of lifetimes ago. Everyone is different.

Perhaps you or I once played the part of those in power. Perhaps we once controlled others, whether in this lifetime or another, and did harm to them or our sacred Earth. We can forgive ourselves, as we forgive them. We can shine our Light upon ourselves and upon them, Love ourselves as we Love them, and not allow those lines of separation to continue within ourselves. Erase them.

Know thyself only by thy truth, the truth of Oneness, the truth of Spirit. The Holy Spirit is the Spirit of Wholeness, and that is who we truly are.

The Heart of Discernment

I've listed just a few of the pieces of misinformation that humankind was subjected to for half an eon. It is now time to use your own heart of discernment, to sift through what you know as "reality" with the heart of higher discernment.

Allow your higher mind and heart, not lower ego, to sift through the information that has kept us confused and in a state of separation and duality. Use your heart to distinguish between what is true and what is not true. Don't spend time questioning and wondering, fearing that your answers might be wrong. Use your heart, your intuition, and you'll be in the right.

This is the process that Mother Mary spoke of, when She told us that She was very careful about what information Jesus was fed as He was growing up. Be careful now about what you are feeding yourself. Read all with discernment.

Dissolve the glue that has held the human-made facts of what is called history for so long in your mind and being. Let those ideas be loosened now, so that they're flowing around you.

When you find one that does not resonate as true, mentally see that idea as coming forward in your mind, to your forehead. Then watch that idea, the energy of it, flow down the back of your head, down your spine, down your legs and feet (or your body if you are lying down), and on into the ground beneath you.

Then envision that energy being absorbed into our Mother Earth. You will still have access to it, can still access that file if need be. But let it go for now, and keep within you what has resonated with your heart as being Truth. Let those new ideas become the foundation of the new you, who is being reborn of Holy Spirit.

Being Reborn

No one need go to a church, temple or other meeting places to find God and the Company of Heaven, though of course you can if you wish. Nor do you need to be baptized again, unless you wish to be. Simply see yourself now as being reborn of Holy Spirit.

This new life requires a commitment to Peace, as the Holy Spirit will not be active in an environment where there is no Peace. Be at Peace, because when you are not in Peace, you are magnetizing and charging the particles around you with a disturbed and negative energy. These particles of God, the photons and essences that surround us, can be charged with what is not Peace. This recreates all over again the karmic path. By attracting that which is not Peace, we are drawing to us more Earthly lessons to wade through, more mountains to climb, until we can again learn to be in Peace.

We can bypass this process. Everything is negotiable in this Earth journey. All of the contracts we make on a soul level can all be ripped up and renegotiated. We have the power to say, "I don't need all that anymore. I don't need the arguments. I don't need the strife. I don't need to support the wars. I don't need the battles, the grudges, and the vengeance. I forgive all, and I'm free, free of all of that." Be at Peace, and the Holy Spirit will reside within you in increasingly joyful ways. There is where your Holy Temple truly is—your own body, your own Earth life, is the Holy Temple of God.

What has come through one of Marina's channelings is that Peace allows Love to grow, and that Love and Peace are Holy Spirit. We can also find Peace in the Divine Masculine, for the Divine Masculine is the God essence of all action.

Being the Holy Spirit

When Divine Peace embodies you in the form of both the Divine Masculine and the Divine Feminine, you will be immersed in Holy Spirit. You will be a Christed being, aware of your Great Mother just as Jesus knew His Mother. You are the brothers and sisters of Jesus, of Buddha, of Quan Yin, of Zoroaster, Kuthumi, Jared, Saint Germain, Melchizedek,

Archangel Michael, and of all the Ascended Masters, the Archangels, the great Light Beings and cosmic beings.

You are their brothers and sisters, no higher or lower than them. The only difference is the illusion of separateness that comes from the illusions of consciousness, the veils of consciousness that only exist in the holographic universe and in this holographic world. We can shed this veil now, by opening up to Truth, Love, Peace, the Holy Spirit, and Oneness.

In this new era, we can take bold steps out of doctrines of misbelief, doctrines of misinformation, and go to the library of the Holy Temple that is within all of us, and read the truth.

Read from a place of higher consciousness, from the pineal gland. Allow your heart to sift through all. Let the two connect, the heart and the pineal gland, the third eye. Know Light and Truth. Find that spark within your eyes as you look in the mirror, and know you are looking at the Holy Spirit, at beautiful Angels, and that all that Oneness is within you.

Honoring the God-Spark Within Us

Know that you can talk to your own Spirit, and that your soul is visible, in the spark in your own eyes. Practice looking in the mirror to see your soul's spark in your eyes. When you have truly seen that, then go into the world and find that spark in others' eyes, meeting your spark with theirs.

You don't have to look all shiny-eyed as you do this, as if you just saw God—that would only scare or disturb people. Do this in a subtle way, so that then when you find a good reaction, you can take that a little further. Then you will know someone whom you can look into the eyes of, and truly say "Namaste." This ancient Hindu greeting means, "The Divine Light within me honors the Divine Light within you" or "The God within me greets the God within you."

In this moment, you are seeing and knowing that the Holy Spirit is within both of you. Then you will be able to say "I love you," whether aloud or within your own being.

The channelings and teachings received in this book are part of an initiation into higher learning that Marina and I have been blessed to experience. I bless you all with the beautiful Divine Love of the Holy Spirit. I bless you with the inspiration to go upon your own path, finding your own gifts and talents, harvesting your own Love, and shining your own Light.

We are brothers and sisters, and we are all equal. Equal in Love and equal in Peace. And so it is.

Chapter Five

The Holy Mother Speaks About Her Life With Jesus

She [the Holy Spirit] says, remind this collective field that they are the open Light of the Christ. That they are a pure being, that they are a miracle.

~ Malachi

From Session L44 on 8.30.12:

Marina: Could we bring in the presence of Mother Mary today?

Malachi: *We shall indeed. Now, beautiful one, allow yourself to feel Her presence. You have asked for Her; She's here. As you feel Her vibrations, feel Her as though She is standing not only in your hearts, but right in between yourselves, supporting each of you, aligning with each of you. Now, beautiful one, what is it you desire to know from Her?*

Marina: We just wanted to feel Her energy.

Malachi: *Can you feel Her energy? For She says unto you this: in the vibrations of your consciousness, you are also carrying the curiosities of Her experience of Earth, in the timeframe of birthing the sacred Son, and Her experiences of the life transformation within Herself, as the beautiful embryonic Energy began to grow into that which has [been] called the Child, the Divine Light.*

She knows you desire of that, and [that] you desire to know of how Her grace of living, while this Child grew, created transformations of the Earth. Would this be true?

Kevin: All of it.

Malachi: *We shall present you with Her words of knowledge. She says unto you, that the entire time that the embryo made its changes into the Child, into the baby called Jesus, Her entire body was a constant flow of Light energy, and She watched it develop by Her inner sight, as well as [by] the natural human body feelings of the great changes that were occurring.*

She says to you, [that] throughout the entire time that is pre-conceptualization of this Child, [and] during the carrying of the Child, of pregnancy, She was speaking with His Spirit. And during this time, there was a constant knowledge of acceptance of what the life growth was going to reveal. And constant information exchanging between Herself and the one to be called Jesus, Yeshua, between Herself and the Divine

Consciousness of purity—[while] knowing that She must maintain a matrix of thought energy and emotional energy that supported the intentions of the great change of humanity, through the agent of the Child called Jesus.

She says to you that as She gave birth to this Child, there was no pain to Her body. There was pure joy in the Light, a blissful Love within Her mind-heart of Her human nature, as well as the blissful knowing of Her spiritual nature, the Spirit of Herself, that knew that this was the moment of a great Earth event, that this Child was born.

She says unto yourselves, that the dear father Joseph was very attentive to this very Light, for He also had the knowing, as you already know, that this was a transforming energy field for the land of the Earth, the consciousness of the Earth.

Now, She says to you, as this Child grew, He grew in much naturalness, as all children grow upon the Earth, and He grew with much naturalness of greater independence. For She says by the time He was able to walk on the land with His physical body, He was constantly wanting to run to sacred places, sacred vortices of the Earth. She says, as a human Mother, She was constantly in chase! [Kevin laughs]

As the Mother of the Spirit awareness, She says She maintained Her knowing the Child was safe, that He would not hurt His human body, that He would not wander so far that He would be harmed by others, about the wildness of Nature. She says, beautiful ones, that She did watch carefully all that was fed to Him. Now, that is not just food. It is languages, words, brought from others, words brought from Herself and Joseph, the [Essene] community.

She tells that the entire community was very aware of how they must speak and share wisdom to and with this Child, so that what was kept in His ears, His conscious and unconscious mind, was the Divine knowing of the Greater Love, and the grand Divine knowing of the grand design of His life, His greater purposes.

She tells you that there are many times in which their life of spiritual realities was to sit with this Child and continue to urge Him to remember His mission, remember His Oneness, and remember how to cultivate that Oneness into the consciousness of Earth. She does tell you that there were no "lost years" of Christ the Jesus—there were none lost. It is only in the concept of humanity that He "disappeared."

Yes, He traveled. He traveled amongst many peoples, and He traveled to the great mountains of Tibet to work with the Masters of knowledge, who would share the essences of Earth intentions and Spirit's intentions, the qualities of higher consciousness that was being used on this Earth. He was searching the peoples that would collectively work together, and He was searching to instruct them [on] how they could call [and create] matrices of Light throughout the Earth.

She tells you there were times when She was in this travel, times when Joseph was in the travel. So the travel is not lost. He was instructing while He traveled, and He was in the learning while He traveled.

Now, why did He return to back home, which you call the Middle East of this day? Why did He return? For there was the intention to anchor Light in that particular pathway of the Earth plane, to anchor Light of the greater truth, and to call the peoples to the domain of harmonic Love.

Now, why? Because, beautiful one, they were carrying some of the greatest separations, some of the greatest angers. You would call it tribal angers, beautiful ones. Tribal angers. Tribal angers, meaning communities divided rather than unified. Cultures divided rather than unified. Philosophies divided rather than unified. And here He chose to bring the words of the Divine, to anchor union and Oneness.

Now She says to you, on this day of your land, on this timing frame of your land, you find your Middle East in great uproar. And She celebrates it. Do you know why?

Kevin: Because of dogmatic belief systems.

Malachi: *Indeed, indeed. To break a paradigm, to challenge a paradigm, that its structure is no longer useful in the consciousness of the advancing souls on Earth. And so where*

there looks to be the greatest disharmony, you will say there is the greatest chaotic creation going on, to break down old paradigms. For that was the center of the old, as well as the center of the new. But the old must break away, must it not? And know within yourselves, it is doing so.

Now, She says you wish to know of Her comprehension of what appeared to be the death of this being Child, and She says this: Prior to Her birth, prior to His birth, prior to what was appearing as a death, She was in total knowing of the Great Design. The great shock, the waves of energy that transformed—She was well aware of what all they meant.

And She says to you, She did not mourn this energy of change. She prayed with this energy of change. She prayed that this vibrational change could occur, for humanity to awaken, to sacrifice their fields of negativity, their fields of separation. She prayed that they would recognize the Christ vibration, not only in this that was called Her Son, but in all Beingness. She prayed with the sacred intent [that] the purpose of the One living Jesus could be recognized by all.

Now, beautiful one, She is saying to you that like waves of ocean that move onto a shore, one wave after another, that you will recognize that this is what has been occurring for 2,600 years. Waves of consciousness, changing. And that which was called the hanging on the cross of the body of the Man called Jesus was not in vain. Not at all. For the waves of the ocean have been creating great changes of consciousness for many centuries, and you of the human race continue to receive these waves, and continue to make changes.

She stands with your hearts, and She says, remind yourselves [that] you are from your heart, experiencing the great wave of changes that is allowing the Christed message of love and Oneness to occur. Yes, within yourselves. Yes, and beyond yourselves.

All right, beautiful ones. Take another breath. [Silence as Kevin and Marina take breaths] *Indeed, does Her message help you?*

Kevin: Oh, it's very, very beautiful. Can I ask a question?

Malachi: *Indeed.*

Kevin: First, I would like to honor Her, in respect to the great Love that She brings to our Earth. I first experienced Her when my Mom was passing from this physical realm. My Mother sensed the presence of Mother Mary and felt peace. She felt love and a lot of comfort as she lived her last days.

Malachi: *Indeed.*

Kevin: I would like to ask, when Mary, Joseph and Yeshua traveled, first to Tibet, when Yeshua was at a young age—did others go with them? Was Thomas, for instance, traveling with them? Or was he someone they met later? Was the one they called John the Baptist known to them as a childhood friend? Did anyone travel with them?

Malachi: *Those of their disciples did not travel with them. That of Saint John did not travel with them. No, they knew that they were not to come together until later. Joseph of Arimathea, he traveled with them.*

Kevin: Yes.

Malachi: *Indeed. For he was a grand traveler, a merchant.*

Kevin: A merchant of tin, right?

Malachi: *Indeed. And so he knew the ways of traveling, and did guide them as they made their travels through the lands that held the sacred vortices, and held the sacred hearts, the ones who would be in the greater Divine service. As you call it, today holders of the Light, holders of the Divine matrix.*

Not only was there the learning and the training and the teaching that was going on, but there was the activation in their mind-bodies, the activation of their center pool of Light, that they would hold Light frequencies, while the great transformation was being brought about as Jesus grew and taught, traveled in His teachings, and indeed was condemned for His teachings.

They have Light frequencies, beautiful ones, so that what could occur was not the burying away of His messages, but the continuance, [the] flow of His messages throughout the world, so that as He would remove Himself from the center of that anchoring change, the messages would nonetheless continue to go forward and to grow.

All right, another question!

Kevin: What would Mother Mary most like me to write about in this book called *The Cosmic Christ,* to get Jesus' truth out, and Mother Mary's truth as well, and also obviously, be a demonstration of Light and Love?

Malachi: *Well, my first answer is coming through the demonstration of Light and Love, and again—what does She do? Well, She brings you back to your heart. She says unto you, the Light of Love radiates through that center, and for humanity to feel the conscious heart means awareness of the sacred vibrations within their heart chakra center.*

With that field of Light that they know and feel within themselves, their own Christed being, their high nature—the resonance of high vibrations that are pure of the Light of the Divinity of oneself.

She says [that] as you tell the story of Jesus the Man growing, that you tell the story that indicates His own knowing of His life course. It was not a secret—not a secret to Her, not a secret to Joseph, not a secret to Yeshua, to the family or to the community. It was not a secret.

It was well known through the Essene community, well known. And because of that, all supported the life events that He had to utilize to cause a great change, a bit of a chaotic change through the field of human consciousness.

You see, beautiful ones, She says you can do a comparison of human consciousness, then and now. Beyond what will be called the Essene grouping, beyond the Tibetans, beyond the priests and priestesses of that which was called Brittany, beyond the chiefs and chieftesses of that which would now be called your Americas, beyond that of the priests and priestesses for which you call the Southern Hemispheres of your world—all of them are holding the matrices of Light, that those in the collective field that held a standard of separation did not realize what was being brought forward to them.

Those that would hold the Light would hold the matrix, would hold the frequencies, were constantly charging the collective field, to take up the message and not lose it, after Jesus would retract His field of living from that which you now call Middle East.

She wants you to tell and look unto humanity, how they will lock themselves into a belief and keep themselves separate from their Christed Beingness, and keep their collective field believing in false informations and living by the false informations.

She says, remind this collective field that they are the open Light of the Christ. And what does that mean within themselves? That they are a pure being, that they are a miracle, and they are a miracle radiating the miracles of changes in their individual qualities of life, and in the collective field of your Earth.

She asks that no one stand to the side and believe that they are limited in their power to express their Divine Self. No one is limited in their power to allow the essence of pure Source to manifest into their desire fields of the Earth plane living. That that is a false information, that they live in separation from the higher truth, from the higher God center. It is a false information that causes humanity to struggle to live from a lower ego, and battle themselves and battle each other, and to attempt to conquer, for one will attempt to conquer another, for one country to conquer another, or one culture conquer another.

All of that comes from the experience of believing that they are separate from the Source, and therefore they must get into greediness and neediness upon the Earth land, to have more, to obtain more, to push out others. That is a fear-based reality, is it not?

And she wants you to tell that to humanity, [that] that [reality]

is fear-based. As long as humanity sits in the component of believing their separation, they will continue to create destructions. They will continue to create groups of people, or single ones, attempting to overcome others.

She calls unto you to constantly remind them, come into the heart, come into the power of compassion, come into the desire of harmony with every single individual component of the Source, so that every single component can be ignited as Light. And then you become creatively resourceful upon this Earth, in a manner that all of you will feel as if you have opened a gold mine, and in the gold mine you are very, very, wealthy.

Wealthy of Spirit, wealthy of mind, wealthy of heart, and wealthy of your physical realm. For She says, the greediness is all about that. "What more can I have? What more can I say that I have? What more can I display that I have?" It is the human desire to have more, and to have more, and to have more. Rather than to unify and realize that you ***have*** *more!* [Laughs]

She says that is what Christ was attempting to teach, as Jesus the Man brought forth abundance in many arenas. He brought forth the abundance of Spirit by what he taught humanity. He brought forth the abundance of health by those that He healed. He brought forth abundance of many things—life, yes, and all of that was demonstration of Oneness consciousness. He brought forth a greater expansion at the human level to feel Love, to channel Love to others, and through the Love, to bring forth all blessings.

Humanity, in its separation, She tells you, does not come from the hand and heart of Love, but the mind only of logic, that says "I must get more, and I must get more." And every day feeling they have less, and they have less, and they have less. No matter how intelligent they are.

For they are not using the heart-mind intelligence. They are using only the mental-mind referencing, the outer reality of Earth. They must reference the inner reality of the sacred heart.

Then the outer reality, of course and always, transforms itself to its greater harmony, its Creator positive reality, and indeed, its greater abundance.

From Session L32 on 1.31.13 – Center Point

Malachi: *All right, beautiful ones, we have entered your realm, and say "Greetings," and with great Light blessings.*

Kevin and Marina: Thank you. Greetings.

Malachi: *We come in with joyful Light, and ask you to feel it bouncing on your hearts, delighting your mind. We may call it tickling your Spirit, could we not?*

Kevin: Very nice!

[Marina laughs]

Malachi: *And as you can feel that bubbling vibration around you, then you can lift yourselves into the joyful time of experiencing communication with the beautiful guardians you have been so closely associated with, have you not?*

Marina: Yes.

Malachi: *Now, beautiful ones, you have been put to quite a lot of work, have you not?*

Kevin and Marina: Yes.

Malachi: *And are you joyful with it?*

Kevin: Very much, yes.

Marina: Yes, very exciting.

Malachi: *Indeed, and that excitement brings up the passion of your soul and the purpose of the Divine. So we call you to delight in it, yes. To dance with it, yes. To sparkle with it, yes. For again, we say unto you in your human form, you are agents, agents that are here saying "Yes" to the grander scheme of consciousness, the Divine, and bringing forward information that can be utilized in your language, so indeed others might learn as well. And all of that is quite important, is it not?*

Kevin and Marina: Yes.

Malachi: *All right now, beautiful ones, we shall begin this day by saying to you, do you wish questions?*

Kevin and Marina: Yes.

Kevin: I can start with one question.

Malachi: *Indeed.*

Kevin: The beautiful Master Jesus said that He was able to attain center point—to center Himself in Peacefulness—in less than a nanosecond or an attosecond, and I am obviously not able to do that.

When He was a Man, when He was embodied as Jesus the Man, whom we know, how did He deal with external things that we all deal with, that people don't like? I know that we can kind of brush some of that off, because they are not in our heart, but sometimes the simplest things in your life are the hardest to deal with. Like parenting, when a child is upset or yelling at you because he or she thinks that you did something wrong. How do you deal with that in that nanosecond? [Kevin and Marina laugh]

Malachi: *All right, all right. Well, beautiful one, we will first give you a giggle, then we will allow the beauty of Jesus the Christ to speak of that, but first, we will remind you to come into your center point, and we call you to take a breath, do we not?*

[Kevin and Marina take deep breaths]

And we say, take a sacred breath. It brings a different connotation to your consciousness and it can help you in being parents. It can help you in working with the different and what you might call, the smaller agitations of life.

You take a moment or an attosecond—very, very, very quick—to take a breath, and in the breathing the intention is to move to center point. Now, to do that takes practice with your sacred breathing. That you breathe and you acknowledge in your inner conscious, "I relax to my center point." And the more you are breathing and stating this, each time you breathe, it will become an automatic alignment in center point. Do you understand?

Kevin: Yes.

Malachi: *Now, from the great Master Jesus, who entered here embodied as Jesus the Man, indeed, there were irritations and agitations that He incurred in a lifetime. And He says to you—and this will give you a good giggle, because He is starting out as Himself as a small boy, meaning His parents had to restrain Him, disciplined Him and direct Him. And He says there were times of great irritation within Himself, when they did not allow Him to go beyond what would be called, as yourselves, the boundary of your yard, and into places and spaces where His soul, His inner consciousness, was guiding Him to go to, so that He could return to his Oneness awareness. And when His parents would become too restrictive, then He had great agitation. Then He says to you, that He would recall who He was—the Divine embodied.*

And He says, He would at that very moment, even as small child, recall that the human condition that He was born into had His family, His community, forgetting the Oneness. And so He had to utilize His ability and center point, to not only recall this reality, but respect it, yet at the very same time, encourage the expansion of the boundaries that were limiting Him from His parents.

Now He wishes you to know that from His Holy Mother, His Holy Father of the Earth plane, when **He** *would recall,* **They** *would recall. And so this is going to be something of a teaching to you: when you recall that you're center point and you're Divine embodied, you will help your child recall, you will help your employee recall, and you will help your neighbor recall. And harmony begins to form.*

For when there is the power of separation, that means [that] you look across the room and you see another person, not simply yourself. That power of separation can lead your consciousness and your subconscious in the sensation of difference, does it not?

When you are in your Oneness moment, that difference is not solid any longer. And the vibrations that you are sending back and forth between each component harmonizes. Then communication opens up, when ones are speaking at your human level, and each will hear the truth of the other, and each can come into a higher regard for it.

Now, He also says to you, beautiful one, [that] there were times in which, as He were a Man, when He felt that He had been explaining and teaching others how to comprehend the sacredness of Love, the harmony of Peace, the beauty of recognizing each individual was indeed Source, and yet continued to find amongst His disciples that they were not fully comprehending.

He says that at times He was agitated, frustrated. And once again, He would return to the center point, by recalling the true Source consciousness, and the division of consciousness that was existing on the Earth plane. And that it was indeed unto His soul passion, to act and to be more in center point in the human condition, so that an imprint could be left for others to follow.

Here we say to you, what do you know you are following of the teachings of Jesus the Christ? What do you know?

Kevin: Well, I know what we are talking about, about staying in center point. I know that He is the Prince of Peace, which brings one to be in a constant state of Peace, to spread Peace, to be without judgment, which He also demonstrated. To forgive, to share, and to have Unconditional Love. And as He also said that He sees the Divine in all, the Divine in everyone, and He also called this Earth "the rejoicing realm, reflecting the beauty of the creative passion and the power of the Divine."

Malachi: *Indeed. Now, beautiful one, that is all you can practice. Practice it and practice it, until it becomes the automatic field of your consciousness. And worry not if this day it's not as perfect, and then laugh and remember, beautiful one, as He has said to you, He had times of agitation on the Earth plane, times when He was discontent in the emotional human body-mind. And yet He also had the very moment to put Him back to center point. Now, He says to you, as He lived in the human body called Jesus, He did come with advanced wisdom, meaning He had had many incarnations already, experiencing the Earth plane to such an extent that He could comprehend the energy of humanity and the energy of the Divinity.*

His intention therefore, as He entered into the body of Jesus the Man, was to unify all of that, and to reveal that unification to all who were willing to hear, and to learn and to gather the vibrations. I say unto you, here thousands of years later, you are all still taking up that vibration of the messages of truth that He brought forth. And the messages of truth that other enlightened masters have brought forth. So you'll take unto yourselves, and we say, we are learning and we are experiencing it more and more. For you are, are you not?

Kevin: Oh yes.

Malachi: *So now, beautiful one, let us do another experience with yourselves, as Jesus is asking of you. When you find yourselves in that discombobulated feeling, where do you notice the distress in your body or chakra centers?*

Kevin: Of course—in the heart center first, and especially, when it involves someone you love.

Malachi: *Indeed, and also notice other centers such as your stomach center.*

Marina: Yes.

Malachi: *Or your lower belly center. Allow yourselves to recall the last moment when you were disturbed. It was not only the heart, you see. Can you recall the energy of the lower belly?*

Kevin: Yes. Yes, I can.

Malachi: *For there, it had a stress point on it. And the stress point between the lower belly and the heart created another stress point in your solar plexus. And so we will say again, beautiful one, the heart, the beautiful open space of yourself in which you want to share, give and receive the Unconditional Love—it was troubled, because you felt you did not give the Unconditional Love you desired. The second chakra* [in the lower abdomen], *beautiful one, is like a soul pain, and the soul pain saying, "Whoops, I forgot!"* [Malachi and Kevin laugh]

And bring that together to the solar plexus. This is another place in the body-mind consciousness that hides and holds guilt. And guilt means you felt bad. And felt bad of yourself.

Well, we want to teach you, that as soon as you can, feel these different energies of your body and know that this is part of your unconscious response through your body. It's the very moment that you turn about and bless yourself.

To bless yourself you can utilize the terms, "I forgive myself, for now I comprehend that I have just had an experience that was out of center point." And when you return to what is termed that Unconditional Love, beautiful one, then the beautiful solar plexus and the second chakra relaxes, and then you take your breath again. You are returning to the center point of Unconditional Love, and something else can occur.

And what else can occur? Now, what if you are in the disciplining of your child?

Well, you'll be able to see what the boundary is in the discipline

that is truly going to support growth, and if it is not all about the supporting of growth, then you will look to the reality and ask yourself, has something occurred here that is truly off balance, and needs to be readdressed?

You see, Jesus is saying back to you, when He was very, very small—that means unto your age frame on the Earth plane, He was about four years old—when He wanted to take that small body further out on a desert where He could be alone, His parents refused it. [Marina and Kevin laugh]

And He felt because the intelligence of His consciousness was so strong, that He was capable of doing that. He was still not used to the human body, and His parents were in very much awareness that He would need food, He would need water, and He would need protection from the strange animals and the insects, and even what could be called badness upon the land. And that in His small body, He would not be able to well defend Himself, because He would not have the strength to do so in the human body. [All laugh]

So He had a lesson to learn. "My body must grow to make the strength of my inner sacred consciousness." And He says, He even then had to recognize that His human consciousness was going to have to grow as well. [Chuckles]

And so, He wants you to know, [that] even in the purification of who He was, He had to learn about the Earth frame of living, and not think simply because His Spirit was quite mature, that His body was.

[All agree, laughing]

Malachi: *So it was appropriate that His parents created for Him a boundary, was it not?*

Marina: Yes.

Malachi: *Does this help you?*

Kevin: Oh, it's wonderful, beautiful. Yes, it does.

Chapter Six

The Birth of a New World

With compassionate energy, send a Light frequency to all of humanity that simply says, Be at Peace, be at Peace.

~ Malachi

From Session L73 on 12.13.2012:

This session occurred before Marina and I were told that Mother Mary is also the Holy Spirit:

Marina: Does anyone want to deliver a message for us?

Malachi: *Indeed, indeed. On this day, beautiful one, what you will feel standing around you, is all of the Great White Brotherhood, all of the great Masters, the great ones, sharing wisdom, presenting wisdom, in what is termed an individual component of energy. In the midst of you, at this very present moment, is the Divine Mother, showing Her striations through that of what is called Quan Yin, and that is what is known unto your humanity as the Holy Virgin Mother.*

Both [are] elements of consciousness, each presenting vibrations in unique patternings. Quan Yin asks of you to feel Her essence, to feel Her patterning of energy, to feel the great compassion. Yes, for She is an agent of compassion. And as you are feeling compassion, to realize that it is a grand understanding of all human nature, as well as Spirit nature, and as the grand understanding of the human nature that you will pass compassion, which is an act of Love to all of humanity, who is standing in a bit of concern of themselves individually, or in their groups of people.

For many, many as they have been receiving these energies of Divine Light frequencies and waves of great Love, great purpose, are still reacting as though they must be afraid of it. And so, with compassionate energy, understanding the complexity of the minds and the emotions of the human endeavor, send a Light frequency again to all of your humanity, that simply says, be at peace, be at peace, be at Peace. [Laughs gently]

The Holy Virgin images Herself with baby Child in Her arms. Now, beautiful ones, it is not Jesus that She is holding in Her arms. She is holding the birthed baby called the New World. She is acknowledging that each one of you on the Earth is a new baby, and from that state, as all mothers do, they hold the babies dear, do they not?

And while they are holding them, they are nurturing them or nursing them. They are bringing the nurturance that is necessary for the healthy growth. As we watch Her image, this picture of the Virgin of the baby, the glow of Light that is all around Her, glows in the symbol of what is called the heart.

And so you will honor it as the sacred heart of the Holy Mother, which also releases compassionate Love. From this, She wishes to honor that yourselves are new-born. And She indeed will nurse and nurture you, as you continue to allow yourselves to walk this pathway, and we shall say to you, the pathway of the mystic ones, indeed diligently utilizing consciousness, emotion and sacred attitude, to merge in Oneness.

Behind the two of them is indeed Saint Germain. And as he stands with them, he wishes of you to realize [that] the essence of his vibrations stands in harmony with the great feminine paradigm. Which does indeed allow for humanity to come to that compassionate state in their own selves, that brings a greater internal Peace, a greater expression of the Unconditional Love, a gentleness that one can turn from one neighbor to another, one friend to another, one family member to another, one continent to another, and lend a hand of Light.

He says unto yourselves, as this activation of energy is impressing in every cell, this is a grand time to continue to feel yourselves, we shall use your term, [as] the "conduit" and we shall use our term, the receptacle.

These great Masters of God have been showing us, in many different ways, the birth of this New World. I know when you look out the window, that the world virtually looks the same. The streets, cars, trees and people are all still there, just as they've always been.

This New World is about a grand change in consciousness. Once consciousness changes, then the outside world will follow.

The unfoldment of this New World, along with the increased intensity of Divine Light being showered upon us, can be quite difficult to experience and adjust to. Our bodies are changing to much more of a Light body. That does not mean that we will glow and fly around. It means that we will be able to absorb more Light. This also means that before this New World began, we have been repelling Light and Divine Love, because we were so deep in the belief of the illusion of this holographic world around us. A world that had been led by an excess of masculine energy, which in turn led to an excess of violence and separation.

Although creation needs the active component of the Divine Masculine to be manifested into what we call our reality, without the balance of our true essence of Peace, Love and Wisdom, the qualities of the Divine Feminine, the world around us becomes a mirror image of our inner imbalance.

We must all find our balance and our center point, with both our masculine and feminine energies. We must also support and nurture every step the Divine Feminine takes to blend into our world.

Imagine an innocent little girl walking through this world for the first time, and seeing some of the atrocities that occur here. Will it be the same in this New World? It is up to us to make it safe. And we can do that by committing to Peace, Unconditional Love, and Forgiveness.

We know that the Divine Mother is not innocent in terms of not knowing what is going on in the world. But She does carry the innocence of a young girl, looking at everything with Love and excitement. This young girl does not live in the past or worry about the future. She is in the moment of truth.

Each of us can do this. Each of us can be in the moment of truth, the now, and appreciate everything and everyone around us, as if we have just discovered them for the first time.

From Session L78 on 5.1.13:

Malachi: *Indeed, and greetings. Greetings and blessings.*

Kevin and Marina: Thank you. Greetings.

Malachi: *And once again, we all blend together, do we not?*

Marina: Yes.

Malachi: *Very good. Now, shall we as always, ask you to take the beauty of your breath. And as you do that, again notice who is present with you, and yes, your new guardian, who steps forward, is here also with us, Zohar.*

And yes, we would give honor to Jesus the Christed One. The beauty of Saint Germain, Zoroaster's presence, is imprinted strongly here.

Marina: Quan Yin is here?

Malachi: *Quan Yin is here, yes indeed, beautiful one. Jared is also here, and shall any others want to place themselves forward, we shall let you know!* [Marina and Kevin laugh]

And so feel their loving greeting to you as well. Now, Zohar spoke to you a lot about wisdom-based consciousness, did he not?

Kevin and Marina: Yes.

Malachi: *And desires to continue that this day, by speaking of the power of your internal self, called the soul self.*

Now, beautiful ones, we would first begin by acknowledging in the beautiful gift of all beings, all essences of this grander element known as the I Am, individuated in souls, [that] every soul of existence is also very much aligned in the wisdom of what we here have been sharing, the evolution of consciousness. The evolution here within yourselves, the evolution of the

Union, meaning the remembrance, remembering that you are the I Am.

So he desires to talk about the soul, its memory release to the personality, the sacredness of the wisdom it carries in honoring this evolution. Are you ready for that?

Kevin: Oh yes.

Malachi: *Here he asks you to allow yourselves the breath that increases your internal awareness. The breath that allows you to feel your sacred holy inner temple. We have spoken to you before about the throne of the soul, have we not?*

Well, we will speak of it again. In the consciousness of the human body, the internal regions of mind and emotion, you have what is called degrees of energies empowered that you call chakra centers.

In that which is termed the second chakra is the states of your consciousness that does indeed carry the vibration of the throne of your soul. So we'll ask you to breathe and relax, into your second chakra. Let us speak about that second chakra, in its multi-dimensional reality of your humanness, and the gateway to your soul.

In the human reality of your second chakra, there are many stations of consciousness that lay here, spin here, we shall call it. They are the processes of your life experiences, in this incarnation and many other incarnations. This section of body-mind consciousness holds memory here of all of that. It holds the memories of the things you can call your passions, desires, dreams. It holds the memories of how in fact you grew and felt accepted or rejected, felt loved or not loved, felt worthy or not worthy. A lot is stored right here.

These challenges of the unconscious that abide here oftentimes are called the very depth of your unconscious fields, but here when we speak of passion, it also is the depth of your passion, your positive creative energy field.

These creative energy fields are used in many ways through the human endeavor that does include creating children. But it does also release the creative consciousness of yourselves. The creativity of your artistry, but the creativity of also living and sharing together.

It is here that the soul creates an impulse, impressing you to take an action, to make a movement towards the ideal goals of the soul during your lifetime. The soul indeed, we say, sits on the throne here, always its majesty always impressing you, to help you move through challenges, recall your reasons for being here, and to remember your sacred self.

It has been the soul impressing you, and the soul impressing all, to release the memories that have kept you locked into separation beliefs, whether through this incarnation or other incarnations that you have explored. The soul has indeed been that guiding force of the I Am, to say all of that was experienced of the past. All of that explored for comprehension, [for the] realizations that have helped guide you towards this time, this New World. And they are now complete, so you may be fresh and new.

Zohar wants you to utilize the greater wisdom of the soul. We will honor it, [calling it] the I Am presence, the existence of that consciousness that is indeed residing in your soul. And when you allow yourself to cross the bridge of the personal self, personal mental-emotional, and enter the beautiful sacred space of the soul vibration, you also enter a great memory, the I Am presence.

And you will feel the memory of the soul acknowledging the power of the great changes, the power of recognizing evolution. And the power to assist you in growing in the evolution of your new states of consciousness. Such power allows you to use the wisdom of Divine consciousness.

Zohar says to you, to consider yourself cultivating your awareness. Now, we'll ask you, as we've talked, what have you felt in your lower belly?

Kevin: For me, it feels almost like a sun there, radiating energy that I can feel which reaches out from my abdomen.

Malachi: [To Marina] *And yes? You?*

Marina: I feel the energy moving and swirling, and that it's warm.

Malachi: *Very good. You have the sensation of the soul vibrational point, do you not?*

Marina: Yes.

Malachi: *Now, beautiful ones, let us have you do this, in the vibration of connecting the throne of your soul to the element of your soul consciousness. Now we are going to ask you to journey with that vibration, as listeners. Well, no—let's first have you as questioners. Give unto your soul this question: "How may I, the personality, cultivate your vibration in this evolution?" Then listen.*

You are going to join the vibration of your soul and you are going to say this: "How might I cultivate the intention of this evolution of consciousness, in my personal reality?"

We leave it at that, for that question. Then we will ask you to feel and hear, listen to your inner responses come forward. All right?

Kevin: Yes. [Silence as Kevin and Marina question]

Malachi: *All right, beautiful ones. What are you sensing?*

Kevin: What I'm sensing is my soul asking to firmly stay in Peace and harmony, and to stay in presence, in the present time. In fact, I couldn't really get it, that Divine time, that split second of no-time—I don't know how to describe it. I feel like the soul showed me a flower, but as a bud, before it had bloomed. It's kind of telling me to be happy, to be the bud, knowing I'm going to be the flower that is going to bloom. To be happy in every stage of that, and let it all unfold, just as a flower unfolds.

Malachi: *Very good. And you, Madam?*

Marina: I felt like my soul tried to tell me that I have to have faith in every day of my life, in everything I do. And it was showing me a soft yellow color. I guess I have to match the vibration of that soft yellow color, which brings great balance and Peace. The soft yellow expands my rays of consciousness, and that is what I experienced.

Malachi: *Very good. Now, Zohar would like to do another level of this you, [with] both of you and with your world. Unto yourselves, are [you] familiar with this term, "anima mundi"?*

Kevin: I'm not.

Malachi: *It is the world's soul. That means all of you, does it not? Here we've asked you to become first in touch with your own soul vibration, for it is important that every individual discovers this vibration within themselves, as this new cultivation is taking shape and form—cultivation of your new selves, your New World, your new birth, as it is.*

Growing in this evolution, yes indeed, you may utilize the beautifulness of your soul's message. Be like the bud and let it flower.

Now we are going to ask you to ride on the stream of vibration that is the soul of your world. We've called you before to be in the collective consciousness. Well, here in the collective soul consciousness, [we're now calling you] to allow yourselves to feel the vibrational message of this cultivation of the higher wisdom, in the evolution of this new state of being.

And [to] allow yourselves to feel that impression that is being brought forth through the individual souls of humanity, and how the collective field is accepting or closing down their ears.

[Silence as Kevin and Marina sense this]

And again—what do you feel and what do you hear?

Kevin: I'm getting that the collective soul is accepting the Light and Love. Perhaps it was repelling the Light previously, but it's now coming to the forefront of the awareness and consciousness of most humans, bringing inner joy. I'm getting that they are excited about it, because most of us have had visions of what we would call idealistic societies, and maybe now people are realizing that those utopian societies are not so idealistic, that maybe they are actually possible.

And as the truth is unveiling and the deceptions are being seen for what they are, then people begin to realize that this world can be a beautiful, loving, caring place for everybody.

And more and more, people are now willing to do what it takes, to be Peaceful, to care for everyone in harmony and Love, and to allow this to unfold.

Malachi: *Indeed, indeed. You've moved right into the wave of them, have you not?*

Kevin: Yes. And of course I understand that there are still little pockets of those who repel the Light. But those pockets are becoming much smaller.

Malachi: *Indeed, very good, very good. And you, Madam?*

Marina: I felt like the collective soul is asking for help, for more help from Lightworkers. That's what I felt.

Malachi: *All right, so here you both have knowledge of what is taking place in the collective soul. The individual components that are continuing to feel the unfoldment of the Light are listening to that [which] is, indeed, "[the] world's soul." That described [as] joyful in the exchange is that which is changing from—here we'll use your term—utopia, from the false belief of utopia to the reality to what truly can take form and place here, as humans harmonize with themselves and do indeed move into the vibration of the true soul.*

Yes, Lightworkers, you are constantly called to maintain your sacred awareness, to lend your vibrations of Light and Peace and Love, absolutely, and the beauty of seeing everyone in their states and stages of harmony.

Here Quan Yin wants to join in on that which is called "realizing the power of the world's soul." For it is indeed an excited, joyful state of consciousness enveloping every soul, with an awareness of what is to come in the power of Peace throughout the world of humanity, and the conscious[ness] of humanity. Quan Yin stands here as a representation of pure compassion.

She wishes for you to see Her, in the vibrational exchange of what is called Divine Mother. When we are speaking of the I Am, it is the pure Essence, undivided. When we begin to speak of the souls, we give honor to the division, and that which is called Divine Father and Divine Mother.

Quan Yin wishes to honor that, from the essence of the Divine Mother birthing every soul. Every soul has always been implanted, imprinted, with the sacred knowing of the I Am, and the beauty and wonder and creative essence in every soul to follow the pathways of evolution.

And here she asks, yes, that you continue to feel in the spiral of the evolution [that] there is a great joy in the anima mundi, the world's soul. There is a great joy, for there is that knowing [that] more Light [and] more Love, radiated, is increasing with every individual soul the awareness of their own empowered state.

She is saying unto you, [that] there is a great impression of consciousness that is not only showing in every individual the power to express their full potential as the I Am. As that is impressed to the world's soul, it is indeed taken up by the individual qualities of the souls, and yes, it will help to strengthen the foundation of Earthly living, that human beings do not have to believe that they cannot come together as indeed the Oneness of Peace, the Oneness of Love.

Every soul is taking up the awareness, as She says. They are taking up the awareness, meaning they are releasing such wisdom from their very essence. [Pause]

Here we are going to tell you another reality. You beautiful beings talk to us very frequently—every day, do you not?

You hear, you listen, you feel, you respond. And so you know of what is called "guardianship." Individual souls in other spheres, dimensions of consciousness, that communicate back unto the Earth. You are also aware of what you'll say [are] human beings who do not realize guardianship is available, [and of] others who indeed would reject it. You are aware of those realities, are you not?

Quan Yin wishes to share with you that through this collective soul of humanity, there is by way of your beautiful Lightworkers, the helping to open the doors of consciousness of more and more beings. Human beings that will sense and feel the guardianships, those helpers willing to assist every individual.

So we are going to ask you both to be aware of how you are finding others newly discovering the guardianships. Do you understand?

Kevin and Marina: Yes.

Malachi: *And yes, for yourselves, we continue to say, listen well, feel well, know well the guardians around you, and encourage all others to listen well, know well, comprehend and utilize the energy information of the beauty of guardianship.*

Now, why does She wish to bring this forward today? Because now, with the gateways, or what you call the "veils of consciousness," much more thin—much more thin—the connection with guardians is much more easy. The impressions in consciousness, meaning thought-forms, from guardians grow stronger every day.

So in the cultivation of your evolution of the world's soul, do we ask you to continue to know that, continue to honor it. For it is the intention of the guardians, the Angelic celestial consciousness, to continue to help the merge of the Oneness consciousness, and it requires Peace in individuals' hearts and minds, does it not?

From Session L69 on 6.24.13:

Malachi: *All right, beautiful beings, we are here present, and yes, in your time and your space, in your matter, we are here present. And in the beauty of the vibration, we ask you to fill up, fill up with the Presence, to let yourselves feel that being filled up with the Presence.*

As we are entering your field, we are watching a beautiful veil of the coloration of pink on this day. Let yourselves feel it through your breath, feel it through your energy. It is loving, it is indeed nurturing, and it is indeed calming. So we'll say blessings unto you, as you receive this vibrational energy. Now we will again laugh with yourselves, for we know you desire your questions first, so if you desire, you may begin in such a manner.

Marina: I have a question about yesterday's session, when I felt Mother Mary's energy. That was such a beautiful, loving energy, and so I felt Her energy even after the session ended.

I felt the desire to feel it and put it on a piece of paper, like I do my channeling.

Mother Mary came through this channeling and right after Mother Mary, Archangel Metatron came. That happened already two times, so I was wondering if there is any correlation. Is Archangel Metatron very close to Mother Mary?

Malachi: *Indeed, indeed. You already have your answer. Very close to Mother Mary. And we shall make another acknowledgement, beautiful one, for both of you, you see. You allowed yourselves to feel Her, you allowed yourselves to sense the unique vibration of Holy Spirit, did you not?*

And you allowed yourselves to know you are open channels for receiving this vibrational wisdom. And so yes, you were impulsed, impressed, and urged to do something with it. That is the gift of your human endeavor. You are feeling the Divine, always. An impulse comes through you—you might call it simply an inspiration to take an action—and when you follow through, something more occurs again. Why?

Because you are allowing, we'll call it, an envelope to open or a door to open, a window to open, a frequency of expanded union, an awareness of it. And yes, when you choose to be colorful with it, when you choose your paintings or your music or your soundings, all of that, you are helping, yes, yourselves—that is quite obvious.

But always, always remember, you are letting the vibration impulse itself to the human field of the collective. Always, what you do affects the whole field.

The beauty here, is that every soul that's existing as a human being on this grand Earth, are indeed in waiting for those very active such as yourselves. But some [are] waiting for the field to impulse them. What a joy! What a gracious joy.

Once again, we shall say, we celebrate your awakening. We celebrate your actions, and indeed, they are very important.

Marina: Thank you.

Malachi: *All right, another question.*

Kevin: I'd like to ask about the books we are working on.

Malachi: *Indeed.*

Kevin: I had a very strong inspiration or impulse, as you say. I came up with twenty-five titles, which will be broken down into five volumes, each containing five books. And I had a very strong impulse and inspiration to release one of the books first, called *The Gospel of Mary the Holy Mother*. [I then changed the title to *The Holy Mother Mary is GOD*]. I just wanted to get your reaction to that, because now that we've learned what we have about Mother Mary's true identity, it becomes apparent that our receiving that information is what has led to my feeling this impulse, this inspiration—is that right?

Malachi: *Indeed, indeed, beautiful one. Your answer came in the moment you learned who this beautiful Divine Feminine is, did it not?*

Kevin: Yes.

Malachi: *And so unto that, the gospel of the Holy Mary, the gospel, which is a directive, is it not?*

It helps humanity learn to remember who and what they are—the individual components of the Holy Spirit—and the beauty of this guidance. Yes, beautiful one, it is important that you initiate that book first.

The following message came to Marina early in the morning of March 2, 2013, from Mother Mary. This part of the message was spoken directly to Marina:

This is my message, dear one. Please deliver today. It is quite important, dear one, quite important. People are losing their uniqueness. Help them to realize they are beautiful, they are special, they are indeed the Love of God. Beautiful one, thank you for bringing my message forward. I am Mother Mary. I love you, dear one. Thank you, dear one! Thank you!

Mother Mary now speaks to all of humanity:

Dear ones, I am Mother Mary. I am bringing you my blessings and Love.

Beautiful beings, indeed this world needs more Love, and I know so many of you are working on it. It is quite wonderful.

Dear ones, bring more Love to your planet. Feel Love for everything that is around you. Feel that beautiful God presence in everything, in every little thing. Everything is so alive and beautiful. Open your eyes, open all your senses, so you can see this great beauty of your world.

Feel it in your hearts. Feel it dear ones, deeply inside you. Feel the appreciation of your existence, the great appreciation of Divine Source around you, appreciation for being a great Divine creation yourself. Feel my presence with you today. I am with you, dear ones. If you are listening to My message, I am with you, dear ones. Feel me in your heart. I am Mother Mary.

Dear ones, share your Love, do Love exchange. It is your natural way of living. Do not close yourself for Love. Love does not hurt. No, it does not. Please do not think that way, dear ones. The true Love of the Divine is always with you in your hearts. Feel how blessed you are, by having this great gift from the Source. It is the Source that is always with you. You are never alone.

You are always loved deeply and forever, no matter what, dear ones, no matter what. Learn how to Love yourself.

You are the one who thinks so often that you are not worthy of Great God's Love. I tell you, that you are so worthy of the Great Love from the Divine.

You ***are*** *Love. You forget that you are Love, playing human games every day. It took you away from the important part of your existence, [the] realization of being a great God creation, of being a pure Love and Light.*

Dear ones, you are indeed the true Love of God. You are all Gods, here on Earth, pretending to be someone else. Great game, dear ones, great achievements. Now it is time to come to the full realization that you are playing the game of human life on Earth. In reality, you are all just pure Light and Love. Nothing else.

Dear ones, Love yourself, Love everyone, Love everything around you, and sing. Sing the song of your soul. You all came here with the beautiful song of your soul. Each one of you has your own unique song. Retrieve that song. It is beautiful. It is yours. It is your gift from your Divine Home. Sing that song every day. It is beautiful. I hear all of you.

Dear ones, every song has its uniqueness. Now realize that each one of you is so unique. Yes, you are, dear ones. It is only your mind that tries to prove that it is wrong. Never mind! You are the child of the Beautiful Divine Source. You came here with Love, and Love loves you. It is always with you. And you are indeed the unique human beings with your own beauty.

Do not compare yourselves with each other—no reason for doing it. You are all like beautiful flowers on the field. How can you compare flowers? They are all beautiful in their own way. Deeply realize today how beautiful you are, how Loved you are, how blessed you are, what a blessed life you are living, dear ones. Contemplate this thought every morning, every day. It will empower you so much, so then you can empower others.

I am Mother Mary. I am sending you my Heavenly Blessings. I Love you and I believe in you. Now your turn is to believe in yourself, dear ones.

My blessings to you. Thank you! I am Mother Mary, the Holy Mother. Blessings.

Chapter Seven

The Holy Mother is Calling for Peace on Our Planet

The Power of Peace is very important, for it is in Peace that Love will abound.

~ Mother Mary, the Holy Spirit,
channeled through Marina

Here is another of Mother Mary's messages to humanity, given to Marina on May 2, 2013:

Beautiful Beings of Light, I am Mother Mary. I am here with you today. I would like to speak to you about your beautiful planet, your Mother Earth.

Your Mother Earth indeed needs your Love and your nurturing care, dear ones. Please join me in my great prayer to bring more Peace on your planet. So many people still stay in that mentality [of] thinking you can resolve a lot of problems by having a war and killing other innocent people.

Why does it occur in their mind? Why, dear ones? Why do you have to think that way?

You know how many wars your planet had—many, and a lot. Please do not let more wars occur on your planet. This is a beautiful planet that needs Peace and harmony. Can you help Her? Can you be a great Peacemaker for your planet? Can you, dear ones? I know you all can, and I would like to help you with this project, Project Peace.

Dear ones, please understand that all of you indeed are connected, even though you act as individual components of the great Divine Source. So when you are all together, working on one great goal—at this time, it is to bring Peace on your beautiful planet—you will be able to achieve it.

Why, dear ones? Because you are so powerful when you are all together. Unite, dear ones, and bring more Peace on your planet. You can start with your home first. Is it peaceful there, or [do] you still have some small battles going on once in a while? Are you all in Peace, or [are] some of you are struggling to achieve it?

Dear ones, it is quite important to find your inner Peace, so you can radiate [that] for others, and become a great example, living your life in a great Peace. Dear ones, you are moving slowly towards your new life. Wars, destructions and disharmony do not belong here. So the quicker you will realize that, and help others to realize that too, the quicker your New World will be here for you.

You are all here together, and you are all creating the effect on the collective human consciousness. So by knowing this, you can change a lot, and much quicker.

This beautiful message of Peace from the Holy Spirit, the Holy Mother Mary, came to my wife Marina, who can hear Her quite clearly. The Holy Spirit can speak through many, including our beautiful Oracle and Marina. There are of course others who receive Her messages, and many more people will now begin to receive messages from the Divine Mother, as well as from other Divine Beings. We all have our own gifts and abilities. I myself have not asked to be an open channel of communication, but to be in blended consciousness with the Holy Spirit and Her beautiful Angels.

From Session 70 on 6.27.13:

Many of the Ascended Masters are mentioned in this session. We will be discussing each of them throughout many books, including one titled *The Book of Masters.*

Malachi: *Today, Zohar will lead the way with yourselves. And as this journey begins, we'll ask you to feel this presence, as you sense the energy of ascending.*

We ask you to note that while you are feeling this energy, you're less aware of third-dimensional reality, and more aware of the multi-dimensional reality. We will ask you to feel the ascent, merging you with the beauty of the Divine Spirit. And today, when we say the Holy Spirit, you know a difference, do you not?

Malachi is referring to what we had learned in the previous session—that Mother Mary is the Holy Spirit. Malachi continues by asking us to enter the Temple of the Ascended Masters, which each of us can enter through our own hearts, in a state of meditation.

Jesus spoke of the Kingdom of God as being inside each of us; this is the same idea. We can enter that holy place in our own minds, inner visions and imaginations. I say "imaginations" because I've learned from these Great Masters that we are living in a holographic universe, and that consciousness has created the hologram by transforming pure energy into what appears to be solid matter.

Humanity has called that consciousness God, and it is. But that consciousness is also of all of us. This reality that we call life on Earth is really our own imaginative manifestation. And yet just as with our Earth, the great temples of the higher dimensions are very real, and can be accessed by us.

Malachi: *And so, you are blended with the Holy Spirit in your ascent. And as you enter the temple [and] come in with such glory, your guardian Zohar and the beauty of the Holy Spirit [are] welcoming you into this realm.*

Here you're first asked to sit in the temple itself, to gaze upon the altar and the lights upon the altar, the beautiful frequency of flickering light, dancing before your third eye.

Each light [is] a flickering blessing. We'll ask you to sit and observe this for a while, but observe in what your world would call, the beauty of prayer. As you are praying, we encourage you to pray for greater alliance with the Universal Truth, that more of yourself is activated in the holiness of who you are.

[Silence]

Feel the Beings of Light who entered the temple with you. The Lord Jesus the Christ, indeed, and of course Saint Germain, Zoroaster and Kuthumi have come forward, Quan Yin [is] present with you. Do indeed notice the frequency of an ancient one called the Buddha, and an ancient one called Moses; they've entered this realm with you.

The Great Masters whom Malachi mentions are named here by their Earthly identifications, drawn from the different cultures and religions into which they have manifested over the centuries. In reality, these are Beings of Light, and there are no lines of separation among them, or anywhere within the Kingdom of Heaven.

That is how it is in the higher realms, and that is how it can be here on Earth. If Buddha, Quan Yin, Jesus and Zoroaster can experience themselves purely as One, then we can do the same. This is what they are asking all of us to do.

Malachi: *Again, we ask you to feel the Angelic Beings, the Light Beings. All are here and present in the celebration, the celebration of Peace. Every one of them is emanating such energy to your Earth, your galaxy, and the galaxies beyond your galaxy.*

Zoroaster becomes very strong in your present awareness, of calling you to come down the hallway. Allow yourselves, once again, to walk through the beautiful hallway and into the Library of Great Wisdom.

In most of the sessions Marina and I have with these Divine beings, we are asked to go to the temple, then to the Library of Great Wisdom. This is a way for the Ascended Masters to get us to leave our lower ego mind and bring our Earth consciousness up to the level of our higher self or higher ego, which exists within the temple. This is where we have a very real connection to these great Divine Beings.

These Beings bring us to the Library or Hall of Wisdom, which contains the Book of Life and the Akashic records. These are written not in solid matter, but as energetic imprints. The Book of Life is a record of every good deed ever performed by anyone, anywhere. The Akashic Records are a record of our souls' journeys, noting everything that has ever been thought, created, spoken, written or experienced, throughout time and space.

By going into a meditative state, coming out of our lower egos and operating from our heart-mind, we are able to access these great sources of information.

The session continues:

Malachi: *Today we are going to use an acronym of the word Peace. Peace: the* ***P****ower* ***E****xpressing* ***A****lways* ***C****ooperatively* ***E****verywhere.*

Feel that power of Peace. Feel the energy called co-operation. Feel it extending through the Universal Consciousness, impressing through the beautiful network of Oneness. Interconnecting sparks of Light, merging in the consciousness of every being, calling forth the co-operation of Peace. [Pause]

Notice this essence of cooperation. Notice how it flows and how it feels, as you recognize its beauty, translating through the essence of all people. Zoroaster is asking each of you to also note the vibrational co-operation of the plant and the animal and the mineral worlds.

So we will quiet ourselves, as you journey with animal, plant, mineral and the humans, to feel them experience the energy of co-operation with the term called Peace. [Silence]

As you're experiencing these individual components, notice their oscillation. Notice in the mineral world, as each mineral oscillates in the power of Peace, how it affects every other mineral throughout your Earth. Allow yourselves to be guided to crystals, that are indeed not only in the iron core, but throughout the world, as you would call it, other human beings are utilizing them.

Here the Buddha is asking of you, to sense the tonality of Peaceful Love in the crystal vibrations. And notice that as you focus on this beauty of Peace, how it indeed creates an oscillation that rings then to every other crystal around your entire Earth world. [Pause]

Archangel Michael now wishes to have you work with his essence and the beauty of the animals. And as you will call [the] animals, you include that which fly, that which swim, and that which crawl—all species.

Here he asks of you to recognize how these animals are hearing the vibration of Peace. And similar to the crystal vibration, as the animals that are wild and the animals that are domesticated are feeling the sense of this oscillation of Peace, notice what they are doing—how their vibrations are taking up the vibration of Peace, and how it helps your world. [Pause]

Quan Yin wishes for you to feel the same vibrational awareness, and the oscillation of Peace, through the plant world. [Pause]

She wishes you to notice how the plant vibration teaches of the cycling of the plant world, that which you would call a life lived, a time of departing, or simply going to such a slow stillness, that a plant can remain dormant through a season and return its vitality in another season. For across your world, there are countries in a different season than yours.

How do these cycles, in the honoring of Peace, assist in this oscillation of transitioning energies? What is the plant world teaching of humanity? [Pause]

And it is Jesus the Christ that steps forward to ask [you] to feel the oscillation of Peace radiating through yourselves, to your brothers and sisters of humanity, to note that one of you sits in the body of male and the other sits in the body of a female, each of you with your own power of yin and yang, and each of you sitting in the bodies of yin and yang.

How do the two of you radiate Peace, and how does this radiation help oscillate the Peace to other human beings? Notice it. Notice that oscillation that indeed emerges from within yourselves, and moves on the wave stream of perpetual Peace to the world. [Pause]

Beautiful woman, you ask how to help your [Earthly] mother. Here in the wave of Peace, send that perpetual energy through her.

Beautiful beings, you are in a library of great knowledge, the library in which, you can say, is the universal consciousness. And let us share something else: these beautiful Masters hand you a blank book. As they hand each of you a blank book, they are also handing you what you will simply call a pen. It is the manner in which you use your thoughts and your feelings.

And you are asked to write in the blank book your present moment knowledge of Peace, and how to maintain the Peace perpetually. Here it is important that you have another knowledge, [which is] that every individual is the script writer, bringing knowledge into the Great Library.

Your world utilizes the term called your 'experiential' experiences. Well, that is what you have in oscillating and riding the waves of Peace. What have you learned, what more have you gathered? What do you feel in yourselves, that you know you will use to continue this perpetual energy? Write it in this beautiful book. Leave it as an imprint for others. [Pause]

The Holy Spirit, the Mother Mary says to you, as you write of Her gospels, comprehend [that] She desires of you to write of the Gospel of Peace and its great importance. You have heard of the written scripture: "Peace I bring to you; my Peace I give."

Let us speak of the importance of this scripture that is now being quoted by the Holy Spirit Herself.

The Prince of Peace did offer us all Peace, not just in the world, but within ourselves. I cannot count how many times Jesus and Malachi have said to Marina and me, "Be in Peace, and fear not."

Jesus speaks of this in John 14:27, when He says to not let our hearts be troubled or afraid. It is one of the great challenges of life, to master the unsettled heart. When we have fear or unrest in our hearts, we need to find Peace, at the root of the problem.

As I write this, our cat Mushka has lost her appetite and is getting thinner by the day. It is possible that she may not survive much longer, though we are trying to give her nourishment by feeding her with a syringe. I feel unsettled and upset in my heart as I think of her leaving us, and am now taking a deep breath into that pain.

I am reminding myself that this is a holographic universe, and that these bodies we're in are not the reality. Spirit is the reality. We Love our cat, but we know if her soul spirit wants to transition, then she will. That is her choice.

We also know that Love never ceases to exist. The Love we have for our cat and our cat's Love for us is everlasting. We have been in contact with many loved ones who have passed over the years, so we know that our cat will be close to us, even after her transition from her body back into the Spirit realm.

We are conducting regular healings for her, but if her soul's choice is to leave, then we must respect that choice as well. We can attempt to negotiate with her soul, but that does not mean that her soul will want to change its course. So we are healing without expectations, while allowing the

Light of the Holy Spirit and Jesus to pass through us into Mushka. That Light may be used to heal, or it may be used just to comfort and aid a being as they transition to the next life. That choice is theirs alone.

I am using a breathing exercise to help me to process my feelings of sadness, in which I take in a breath while saying the word Peace four times. This method was suggested by Quan Yin in one of our sessions.

I am blessing Mushka and her choice with the fullness of my Love. I am visualizing her being always at Peace, and visualizing myself being always at Peace. I am feeling the pain and the heartache being released. I feel my heart open to the Love of the Essence of Holy Spirit, and that feels very comforting, though I am tired from the entire experience.

Death—the fear of it, and the fear of losing loved ones to it—are large mountains to climb on the path to total inner Peace. I have my backpack and my hiking boots on, and I intend to reach the summit. I may slip and travel off the quickest and safest path, but I will pick myself up, find my way again, and up that mountain I shall go.

Prayers for assistance will always bring my guides into action. The Angels that are around me and all of us are here to help. But they cannot come forward and help us until we ask.

* * * * * *

It is now three days since I wrote the preceding paragraphs, and Mushka is no longer here with us. But we received a wonderful gift, as Jesus and the Great White

Brotherhood brought Mushka's soul to Marina. Marina was able to speak with Mushka's soul, and when I read the information below, I was climbing high on the mountain, to a summit that I will call Inner Peace.

The following message from the Great White Brotherhood of Light was received by Marina just before Mushka transitioned to the next life:

Brotherhood: *Greetings, dear one. We are all here with you now, experiencing what you call emotions. Yes, we feel your emotions about your loving cat. Yes, she feels as [if] she is going to pass. Dear one, give her Love; she is leaving. Her body can no longer hold the spirit. She is weak.*

Dear one, you can take her to the vet, but it will only help her for a few days. The soul is ready to depart. Dear one, we shall say to you this; let her rest, and let her die in Peace.

Why does the body need to suffer so much? It is much easier to make a transition [that way]. Her beautiful soul desires to leave her body. She is ready to leave this planet. She will come back to you again, and she will stay longer this time.

Dear one, accept the natural process of life. Life did not end for her spirit. She is a great cat, and she got enough Love from you. Now, it is her time to leave this planet.

Marina: Can you give her many blessings of Love?

Brotherhood: *We will be holding her in our arms.*

Marina: Do we need to do any ceremony when she passes?

Brotherhood: *Pray for her soul, to make a smooth transition.*

Marina then asked the Brotherhood if she could speak to Mushka's soul. They answered:

Brotherhood: *She is saying to you:*

> Dear one, my time on Earth is over. I had a great life with you, although it was short. I thank you for all the Love I received from you, and I will see you all soon. I will be back on Earth quite soon. I will intend to have a longer life in my next incarnation. I feel excited and happy, although my body will not show my excitement.
>
> Dear one, do not cry. Celebrate the freedom of my spirit from the body that no longer has life to provide. I am happy now. I will come back soon. You will see me again as your loving cat. Take your time to choose another cat for your home. I will be with you very soon.

Marina: Are you going to be in a female body again?

Yes, I will be in a female body again, with blue eyes. That is how you will know me. Thank you, dear one, for being such a great parent for me. Thank you!

Mushka was born on December, 19, 2012, and died on August, 20, 2013.

Marina writes:

Early in the morning, Kevin told me that Mushka had passed away. I started to cry. It was hard to hold back my tears. She was such a loving little cat. She was all Love. She was always very Peaceful. So I decided to see if I could speak to her soul. The night before, while I was healing her, I'd received a vision of her soul.

Later that day, I felt a strong intention to paint what I saw. I painted half of the vision. I haven't seen the other half yet. I will receive it soon in my meditation time.

I also asked the Great White Brotherhood if they had anything to say about our cat Mushka.

Brotherhood: *Dear one, she is fine. She has finally got released from her body. Her body was quite ill, and no longer could provide the quality of life for her spirit.*

Dear one, we are celebrating her birth here. She is a beautiful being, full of Love. She will be back with you quite soon. She is saying to you:

> I am waiting for my new body, so I can reunite with you again. Wait for me—I am coming very soon. Next month or so, I will be in my new body. As I said before, my eyes will be blue and I will have a very white fur. I will be your White Light Cat.
>
> My soul will be going through transition, which will allow me to go on the different level of my soul existence. I will be with you very soon. Please do not cry, and please celebrate my rebirth. I am with you now in spirit. I am your Spirit cat. I know how much you loved my body and my personality. You will receive it again and much more.
>
> Thank you for taking care of me and my body. I received a lot of Light and Love from you. Thank you to you all. I will be in a much healthier body next time, so I will be very playful, and will provide a lot of fun for you to enjoy me, as your new old friend!

Marina: I felt her soul was smiling, and I felt how sweet she is, and how happy she is, and that made me happy.

Jesus has told us that He always maintained Peace within Himself. He did this not only because He was a Divine Being, but because as a human, He understood that we are all of the One Source, the Holy Spirit, and that Source is ever present within us. He knew that Inner

Peace was necessary for maintaining awareness of our connection to that Source.

He understood that this Earth is a hologram, an illusion. That what is real is the Love that is in our hearts and the part of each of us that is in everyone else. He knew that not the life of this hologram, but the life of the Grand World of Heaven, is eternal. He also knew that a troubled heart shrouded in fear is one that is separate from Love, its true essence. Belief in this hologram can possess us, causing us to spin webs of chaos out of fear, worry and doubt.

John 14:27 speaks to this: "Peace I leave with you, my peace I give to you: not as the world gives, give I to you. Let not your heart be troubled, neither let it be afraid."

John 16:33 also speaks of Peace: "I have told you these things, so that in me, you may have peace. In this world you will have trouble. But take heart! I have overcome the world."

Jesus is saying that there is Peace in the Christ consciousness. Jesus the Man did overcome the strife of the world. He mastered the Earthly existence and created a blueprint for all of us to follow. He does not want to be followed in the sense of being placed on a pedestal. He wants us to follow his example, of being a Christ with Christ consciousness.

Jesus the Angelic Divine being is the Godhead of Christ consciousness, which means He is within all of us. When we actualize our Christ consciousness, we are blended with Him, whether we have called ourselves Christian or not.

Jesus is also letting us know that this holographic

world is designed to be troublesome, and that the path of the one seeking to be enlightened is to not engage in the trouble of this world. As Malachi says here, the path of enlightenment is a path of Peace.

The session continues:

Malachi: *This has been the active scripture of your lesson today. The mineral world, the beautiful animal world, the plant and the human world, oscillating in the energy of Peace, oscillating in the energy of the Holy Spirit.*

The Power of Peace is very important, for it is in Peace that Love will abound. When Peace is not known and not felt, ones do not come to their center point and allow Peace to open the doorway of Love within themselves. She [Holy Spirit] asks of you to contemplate how Peace and Love are important components of the Holy Spirit. [Pause]

Feel the blessings of the wise ones, of the Masters. Feel the blessings of what you have written in your own book. When you return to the library, remember your book is there. Whenever you desire, re-enter the beautiful library and imprint your book with more knowledge.

Allow these Great Masters to take you from the beautiful library, once again down the hall and into the temple. Once again, as you are then in the temple, give honorage, gratitude for the great Love [and] expanded wisdom in the power of Peace. [Pause]

Allow yourselves again, to remove yourselves from the temple, meaning to descend back into the matter of the third-dimensional reality that you are [returning to]. And as you begin to feel yourself more collected in your third-dimensional consciousness, notice how you feel the Peacefulness within you. [Pause]

Breathe in, exhale Peace. Breathe in the Peace and exhale the Peace, and know you are Peace. Then as you allow yourself back into your third dimensionality, you may speak of your experiences. Vocalize it, [so] that you solidify it. [Pause]

Kevin: Well, I'm going to start with saying that I'm feeling the Love from the Holy Spirit, the Holy Mother, and understanding that if we don't have Peace, we don't truly live that Love.

The moment we don't have Peace, we form an illusion. We go off into an illusionary state of mind, an illusionary "reality" that's not a reality, with the whole purpose of learning to be in Peace. Then we can get back to that one moment of being so close to Holy Spirit that we are living in true Love, and true Peace.

One of the books we're writing is titled *Be in Peace.* I've written a lot about that subject already, asking people to create a sphere of radiance around them, where they are always in center point, where they always find Peace within that sphere around them, to create a beautiful Light there, and to invite in all the Masters—so that you [Malachi], Jesus, Saint Germain, Quan Yin and Zoroaster—everybody, at any time, can enter this sphere.

I then suggest that people open their own sphere and see where the shadows are, and shine their Light upon the shadows, so that we are individually surrounded by our own Light, our own Peaceful center point.

I understand that we can have a Heaven on Earth, by living and embodying the Holy Spirit, and sending it out, radiating the Holy Spirit.

Regarding the yin/yang, masculine/feminine balance—it is possible to create Peace from male energy. But if you reverse that, you obviously get aggression. So it's very important to curtail that masculine energy, and to understand that the male way of thinking, of conquering, expanding and progress, can still happen, but in Peace. In a way that blends with all nature, with all people, all animals, and all minerals. We can build a beautiful world, out of that Peaceful state.

During this session, I also felt myself stepping into the body of Jesus, and feeling the wonderful energy of Peace that He brought and still brings to the world. And with that, I felt that Zoroaster—as we once called him, the Builder—taught us how to bring the essence of something that's not in matter into our eighth chakra—creating that and bringing that down to our second chakra, and then running that energy back and forth, so we can manifest it.

That is what I was partially attempting to do—manifest that Peace from the Source of Peace, which to me would be Jesus and Saint Germain. And bring that into my second chakra, and try to bring that into the world.

Malachi: *Very good, very good. And you, beautiful woman?*

Marina: I also felt that Mother Mary, the Holy Spirit, helped me to feel it very strongly. I have been noticing this, because I have been working on bringing Peace into my body.

The Peace and the Love of the Holy Spirit feel the same to me. So I felt that great Peace that for me is the presence of the Holy Spirit, and that feeling that Peace and sending that Peace to everybody is helping to bring in the essence of the Holy Spirit here on Earth. We can do that through the minerals, the plants, and the animals, and for human beings.

When I radiated Peace separately, to the minerals for instance, I heard them thank me for that, and they were absorbing it and spreading it amongst each other. For the plants I felt the same, and for the animals, too.

I know that the domesticated animals, for example, like our

cats, carry that vibration, because when I go and spend time with them, they do radiate that Peace. I often go there to get that focus of Peace and healing from them, because they carry that Holy Spirit Love and Peace.

What Mother Mary taught us, is to put our left hand on our heart, and to extend out our right hand. This is one way I try to radiate Peace and Love. That's how I experienced that. So if everybody feels that Peace, they'll feel that wholeness, like the Holy Spirit. That's what I experienced and what I felt with the Light.

Malachi: *Very good, very good. To each of you we'll say this: you will also decide here that you may pick up your crystals and oscillate in the vibration of Peace, and let there be a radiance of that consistently. And as you are presenting crystals to your Earthly mother, it is not only a crystal of healing, but impregnated with that of the vibration of Peace, you see.*

So into yourselves, you can utilize your own crystals to be programmed with great Peace. You can feel the oscillation of them throughout the Earth. They are already hearing it, they are already feeling it. Now when you bring an intention right along with it, you increase it. Do you understand?

Yes, indeed, it is very important that the radiance of Peace is the occurrence of consciousness here, that indeed, the beauty of Love can be the existence. As you already know, you're in a New World of compassion.

Compassion carries with it Peace, carries with it Love, and carries with it Harmony. Yourselves, yes, you're agents of Peace, and Love, and Harmony, and you're learning well the beauty and the power of Peace.

And it must be expressed through all, and all must cooperate everywhere. Cooperation of this oscillation needs to occur, so that the human race can live in Peace, radiating Peaceful Love, and opening themselves to greater qualities of creative inspiration.

For the Divine, in the cultivation of its New World self, does indeed need the co-operation of the individual components with the freewill and choice. So [that] the intention of the New World of compassion, [the] New World of Peacefulness, occurs with a grace, not a struggle.

All right, beautiful ones. Once again you've learned another lesson of Peace, have you not?

Kevin and Marina: Yes, thank you very much.

Malachi: *And from this beautiful group of Masters, receive additional blessings always. Take the presence of Peace and expand it constantly. Then we are complete this day.*

And you are beautiful beings of Light. We thank you very much, and of course, we leave you with a blessing. Peace be with you.

Kevin and Marina: Thank you.

Chapter Eight

The Mystical Christ, Our Center Point

Jesus says to you, "Do not place me on a pedestal. Feel me beside you. We are equal." Feel yourself be [the] equal of Christ.

~ Malachi

Here Malachi relays information from Saint Germain, about the Christ consciousness that many are beginning to experience:

From Session L55 on 6.7.2012:

Malachi: *Allow yourselves to blend with him [Saint Germain] and learn of the emerald. And why is he bringing you the emerald, you see? Because it has sacred properties for this New World, and what we will call the new generation of the emeralds, for that is something else for you to learn.*

There are new generations of that which is called the crystals, and the beautiful stones of your Earth, for they are already rising out of the foundation of the New World, encoded.

Here we shall tell you this: Saint Germain has already been impressing unto your consciousness the desire to have you write the book, and write the story, and write a wisdom. Do you understand?

Kevin: Yes, and we are getting that.

Malachi: *Indeed, you are. And so this is part of it. So allow yourselves, yes, to maintain meditation times, union times, [so] that you hear, you feel and you channel the information. Again, important, mark that in your mind-heart.*

Kevin: Yes, we will.

This session marked the first time that Malachi, Saint Germain and Jesus asked one or both us to write a book. I have written almost every day since then, and now have hundreds of pages of writing. Those writings will appear in the many books to come.

We speak to these Divine Beings every week, and every week there are new revelations. Originally, I'd thought this book was going to be about Mother Mary talking about Her life with Jesus and Joseph. We were fortunate to receive one gospel from Mother Mary, speaking about that Divine lifetime on Earth.

At the time that the Holy Mother gifted us with that session, we did not know that She was the Holy Spirit. This book then proceeded to take on a life of its own—you could say, a life blended with these great Divine Beings.

In the beginning, when we first started with Malachi, we would ask which books contained the greatest truth. I didn't realize at that time, that we were speaking to the same great Divine Beings that have been written about in so many scriptures and spiritual books through the ages.

Many great books such as the Bible do carry the words of these Divine Masters, but they are also speaking to us now, in our modern era. We can ask them anything, and they seem to want to tell us everything. This is a miracle, and one that we will always share with the world.

The session continues:

Kevin: Is there something that Jesus would like us to do or be aware of?

Malachi: *Indeed, He tells you this: this is the time of the mystical Christ rising in every being. To know that within yourselves is to continue to maintain its sacred awareness within your beings, to live as though you know, feel and recognize His living stature.*

It is an all-heal[ing] stature. It is indeed a loving stature. It has always been the same message: you are the Divine, and it is important to know it.

For the I Am is not separate from you. And He was one of the first in evolution to be able to announce that very clearly. Do you understand?

Kevin: And we thank Him for that, and we do understand that. I believe He said, "I Am the resurrection. I Am the Christ."

Malachi: *Indeed. He also says, listen for Him. He'll speak to you. Listen for Him. He will help you in your healings.*

All right, ones. And so yes, continue to make your mark in union with the Masters. Continue to make your awareness with the union you have with the Masters. Jesus says to you, "Do not place me on a pedestal. Feel me beside you. We are equal." Feel yourself be [the] equal of Christ, do you understand?

He is not lessening His energy to be beside you. He is you. You are He. As you are Saint Germain, as you are the God force, as you are the I Am—all of it is the same. Now you are discovering it more and more, within yourselves.

Before we move on to the next session, I would like to introduce you to Ascended Master Jared.

We met him in a very interesting way. During one of these sacred sessions, I asked if there was any Master whom Marina and I had never heard of before, who would like to come forward. That is when Jared stepped forward, with his gentle and beautiful energy.

I will release that particular session in another book, *The Book of Masters*. Until then, I will share one great revelation about Jared. I asked him when in our time frame did he make his ascension, which is a sort of graduation from the Earthly karmic wheel. He said it was 598 BCE. I than asked him who was the first to greet him as he entered the Kingdom of Heaven. He said it was Buddha and the Christ, the one we know as Jesus.

This occurred almost 600 years before the life of the Man, Jesus. This revelation is very important for understanding Jesus, and we will go deeper into this in the upcoming book, *Jesus, the Prince of Peace.*

From Session L28 on 1.5.12:

Marina: We haven't talked to Master Jared for a long time, so we just wanted to honor him, and everyone else. We would like to speak to him, if he wants to say something to us.

Malachi: *All right. We have invited his presence to come forward, out of the circle of the [Great] White Brotherhood [of Light], and as he does, he comes forward joyfully. As he does, he also gives indication that he has been remaining with you, not separate from you. So do indeed, know that from his conscious state, as well to your conscious state.*

Marina: Thank you.

Malachi: *As he is coming forward, beautiful ones, he is also coming forward with more of the messages of what you have heard this day, [regarding] the beauty of what your energy called your home, is doing presently.*

Now Jared says to you, inasmuch as your vibrations are light frequencies that attract souls, so it is [that] if you were to extend your consciousness above the Earth, looking down to that which is called the building of your home, you would find that it is radiating [a] Light frequency. Yes, we know this is part of the vortex in which you are living upon, yet he wishes for you to realize it is what you are doing within the home.

For you are creating resonant rays of Light that are penetrating what is called your building, the home, and indeed, [they] become [a] beacon of light, again to humanity and throughout your galaxy.

So this is why he says, allow yourself to slip out of the body-mind consciousness, and into the ethereal Heaven. And you can peer back upon your Earth to your home, and you will see it as though it is a dome of Light. Within that, he says to you, that vibration is being felt throughout your Earth and, it is said, throughout the galaxy.

He also wishes for you to realize that in the vibrational intentions you have of your minds and your hearts, you are saying to the galactic brothers and sisters, we are way-showers, and we are willing participants in the interactive qualities of dimensions.

You are indeed, as though a beacon of Light that says to the galactic brothers and sisters, enter our realm. We are humans, ready to meet other souls of other dimensions, galactic consciousness. We are souls that are willing to join forces with those who have explored more than us, and those who wish to explore similar to us.

Jared tells you this: You too, indeed, have walked into a passion of your own souls in the evolution of your soul consciousness, to express more of the higher intentions of wisdom, to express more [of] the Christed essence, and it is noticeable, noticeable to all.

Jared is also saying this to yourselves: Continue the writing of this knowledge, the sharing of it, and continue to allow yourselves to find ways that may bring it about in art forms.

Know the impressions that you are giving. Feel the impressions you are receiving. Jared is asking the two of you, to feel the pressure upon your shoulders that is the pressure of touch, the pressure of touch. It is the touch of a companion. That is his touch.

Kevin and Marina: Thank you, Jared.

Malachi: *And he presents a question. How are you recognizing your human union with your spiritual realms?*

Kevin: I'm feeling the vibration. I'm feeling part of it. So that I feel to be a minute little particle within a great universe, then I feel the wholeness of my being, which is my Lighted, Christed being. I guess the Christed awareness means to understand it, have a conscious awareness of it, and possibly even to command it.

Malachi: *Indeed, indeed, indeed. It is beautiful that you note that you can command it, for in that regard you are recognizing [that] to command is to bring something into manifestation. To take the radiance of the ethereal vibration and bring it forward. To live it, as we call it, to live it. What more each of you are feeling? What more of the Light frequencies are you aware of?*

Kevin: Marina and I have both said that we're starting to notice every object, and everything around us, that it has its own Beingness. When I look at most objects, I can see a little happiness and Love in each object, in each thing, each being—mostly things, because I'm in a room right now. But when I'm outside, it's also the trees, the leaves, the grass, flowers, water and air.

Malachi: *We celebrate an acknowledgment with that awareness you are having. What you are allowing yourselves to do is to blend into fourth-dimensional experience. Not be separate from it. But you are blending with it.*

You are feeling the vitality of everything, its flow and its frequency, its joy of consciousness that brings you into unification with your fourth dimension, and indeed, of Holy Spirit. As you are feeling the Love, you feel it greater and greater. This will bring you more into the fifth and sixth dimension as well.

Jared says, "Rejoice, rejoice!" For this is when you will allow yourselves to truly utilize your Christed Beingness. For the beauty of the Man known as Jesus walked in all dimensions, and utilized very much the vibrational essence of the fourth dimension, in which the structural parts of all things are, [as] you call it, "the atoms in motion."

Jesus could feel and notice when they were in the imbalance. And [by] blending with the art of Love—the consciousness of Love, the beingness of wholeness—[He would] bring them back into their harmony, and thus the healings occurred.

Here Jesus wishes to tell you, that the more you are able to do this, the more you feel the harmony, you can bring [it] to the atom aspect of your whole collective world.

The participation in which, this day, you were asked to feel your center point in [the] holographic vibration, and return to the individual point of yourself, is to know this grander harmony. For every individual component that truly lives this harmony, of course, [resonates with] the beauty of every other individual component, calling it back to the center point. The I Am is calling it all back to the One harmony.

As always, we will always use the power of the words "free will" and "choice." But ultimately, know that within individual components, the ultimate free will is to will the individual components into the awareness of Oneness, the Whole Being.

It is an honoring to you again, for [that] which is called your intentions, to make such [a] blend of awareness, such recognition of the frequencies of vibratory joy in all things. [Laughs] *Again, we say that is beautiful.*

Marina: Yes.

Kevin: Very beautiful.

Malachi: *All right, another breath within yourselves. Now, beautiful ones, you are in heightened sensitivity, are you not?*

Kevin and Marina: Yes.

Malachi: *Very good. Now what we are going to ask yourself to do, is as you sit in the very presence of one room of your home, to recognize the beauty of sensitivity you have with your home environment, beyond the room. And what are you sensing?*

Kevin: I definitely feel a Peaceful energy as I float through the house. Almost like there are flowers everywhere.

Marina: It feels like there are so many beings in the house.

Malachi: *Indeed, indeed, very good. There is the Peacefulness, that is what you are activating. There is the joy of many beings. For again, that is that which is called the Allness in its beautiful individuated components of the Angelic realms, the Masters. And it is indeed the souls that are transferring to the Earth from the non-Earth, [and] from the non-Earth to the Earth. It is a blessing.*

Marina: Thank you so much.

Malachi: *Indeed, indeed. Well, beautiful ones, it is time for us once again to leave the body, is it not? And so, we leave you in the center point of the Light, in the beauty of your sensitivity. And we will indeed remind you to remain contained, that you are not knocked off of your balance, that you have the perfect recognition of the harmonious Love of all.*

All right, beautiful beings, then we do leave, in the center of Peace and Light, and the center of the I Am.

Marina: Thank you so much.

There are several ways to find our center point. We

know from what has been revealed in this book that we must keep our hearts in Peace, without struggle and fear. But how do we do that, as vulnerable beings in a dualistic, unpredictable world?

One way is to master our "I Am" presence, so that we can command the world around us and manifest our dreams. Remember that the I Am presence is the presence of the Holy Spirit within us, that because we are all One, we all have the opportunity to be God, and can command and create like God.

When I say God, I am referring to the Holy Spirit, understanding that the Divine Mother created the Divine Father. The Divine Father is the active essence of the Holy Spirit, bringing forth worlds of physical matter.

When the Divine Father manifests the Divine Mother's creations, those creations are all Sons and Daughters of God. Within the holographic universe, God takes on three aspects: the Mother or feminine aspect of God, the Father or masculine aspect of the creation principle of existence, and the Son, which is the creation or all existence.

That is the three in one, the triangle with the three aspects, which together are the Holy Trinity. They are the grid that defines the integrity of life in this holographic universe.

The grid can also be seen as a Diamond Grid, containing the Divine DNA and RNA of Source. This is not biological DNA and RNA. It is Source DNA and RNA, which carry the codes of perfection for all existence. I will talk more about this in our book *Jesus, the Greatest Healer*.

We know from science that we are all energy, that matter is not solid at microscopic levels. The energy that we are made of is God, and God is never separate from us, even when we separate our consciousness from God. We are all made of Source energy; we are all made of God. Now is the time to understand that, and more importantly, to trust it.

Trust is what we need in order to master Inner Peace and to stay in center point. Trust that our Mother is always there, with a huge heart and open arms. She is the safety net for all, because we are eternal beings of Her spiritual body.

Her Sacred Fire, Her Light of Source gives us life, and keeps our hearts beating within this holographic universe.

Love your Divine Mother and trust Her in every way, and She will guide you with every Divine breath that you take.

Chapter Nine

Mother Earth and the Christ Consciousness

> *For now is a time that your world is in great challenge, but at the same time, your world is in great healing.*
>
> ~ Malachi

The following is an excerpt from our upcoming book, *The Sacred Life of Joseph.* Below is one of the questions I asked in trying to understand the Divine Masculine or Divine Father.

From Session L77 on 7.11.13:

Kevin: So, why is there a Godhead for the Divine Feminine, and not one for the Divine Masculine? It took a while for me to even get to the point of establishing that there is not one Person whom you could say is the active consciousness, or Godhead of the Divine Masculine.

Malachi: *Beautiful being, the Divine Masculine is the active essence of the Divine Feminine. The active essence of the Divine Feminine. Everything that emerges from the Holy Spirit, therefore, is the Godhead. For it is the action of that individual component of the Holy Spirit.*

So as you heard Saint Germain say, "I am the Godhead. You are the Godhead," you've also heard the same from Jesus the Christ. And as you study all [the] Masters, the same is said. And so yes, you shall try and try and try to name it, but you'll not find the pure name, you'll not find an essence of a Being that you can say, You are It!

Because the It-ness—we'll call it the It-ness—is the Everything. And the Everything is the Holy Spirit. And the Holy Spirit is the Divine Feminine vibration.

From Session L46 on 9.26.2012 - Living the Christed Awareness

Malachi: *Unto here, the first One to bring forth a message to yourselves, is that One you know as Jesus the Christ.*

In His presence here with you, He wishes to continue to ask of yourselves, [to] be in that Christed Light of your inner center. He is acknowledging within all of you the intention of sacredness, that you are carrying a desire to continue your growth of your

Spirit consciousness, to have your Spirit consciousness fully activated in your daily routines.

He says to you here now, feel yourself Christed in your center. When you allow yourselves to let your mind move inwards and feel your own Christed Beingness, you are activating a vibration in which you will find yourselves Peaceful, confident and able.

Now, "able" means many things. Able to maintain the health of your body, He says. Able to continue to radiate Light into the frequency of collective consciousness, for the healing power that is indeed in the waves of change. He is asking of yourselves to stay stable in such Light. "Stable" meaning "consistent." Do you understand?

For now is a time that you can see your world in great challenge, but at the same time, your world is in great healing. And at the same time, your world is at the point of allowing what is called the coming of the Christed Being within each other.

He is again asking that during your meditation times, you begin with a visualization that the essence of your humanness recognizes as Jesus the Man. Then, feel yourselves, again and again, blend to that vibration within yourselves.

In your meditation time, consistently ask of His presence, the presence that encourages you with more knowledge. More knowledge of living Christed, more knowledge of living your Christed Self. He is honoring your essences, for your intentions to live the Christed Beingness.

Yes, He does say that working with you, working with Saint Germain, there is the intention to continue the message [of] how to live Christed. How to live your Christ awareness daily, hourly, moment by moment. And with the acknowledgement, beautiful ones, we shall say this: How are you feeling, with your Christed Beingness?

Kevin: I feel really good with it. I spend a great deal of my day thinking, being part of it, and meditating, reading, typing discourses and listening to these sessions, going into meditations and finding Peace within my heart, finding Peace with everybody around me, and it's been great.

Marina: It helps me to feel more and be more dedicated to my Light work.

Malachi: *Indeed, indeed, indeed.*

Kevin: I am experiencing what we talked about yesterday. I think that some of the memories or emotions, stuff that might be stuck in the emotionality of my being—those memories are being cut and being released. And they have to go through me.

Malachi: *Indeed.*

Kevin: I am doing what you told us yesterday, and that is to bless the emotions and memories, to give them Love and Light, and let them go.

Malachi: *Indeed, indeed. The more you are doing that, [then] the more you are allowing your Christed Beingness to be center point. Know that, and know that this being, coming to you as Jesus the Christed one, is acknowledging these changes within you. Realizing, recognizing—that is your better word—recognizing how you are allowing yourselves much more of the Christed Light to be in the frontal part of your consciousness.*

Not simply where you find it when you are in your relaxed, meditative state, but the quality of living it. This too, we would say to you, is why His presence is so very strong here, on this day. It is an honor and a recognition. Do you understand?

And here, yes, we will repeat: He will encourage, continue to encourage [with] messages. Messages to be brought forward in your conscious states that remind you of simple affirmative authorities of living the Christed way. Continue to write them, for you will continue to share them, and this is important.

From Session L57 in August 2012 – The Activated Pineal Gland

Kevin: When Jesus—Yeshua Ben Josef—walked this Earth, did He have a fully activated pineal gland?

Malachi: *He did indeed, and it was noticed at His birth. He had what you call the purest open channel. In the human form nature, He had that vibration open unto Himself, that He was giving Himself recognition, "I am the Oneness. I am the Source. I am the Christed Being." In your world, you call Him the Messiah. Well, you may utilize all of those names. He already knew that at His birth.*

Kevin: Wow!

Malachi: *It was seen very clearly by His parents—mother, father—Mary, Joseph—do you understand?*

Kevin: Was Joseph Saint Germain, incarnated?

Malachi: I*ndeed, indeed. Now unto yourselves, did you not already know that?*

Kevin: Pretty much, yes. I just didn't know the biology of it, if you want to call it that.

Malachi: *Indeed, indeed. For yourselves, this would help you to know this. Because in Jesus' temple called the body, the pineal vibration was a very open channel. He did indeed realize how He was receiving, meaning allowing to receive in the human mind, the energies of the Divine Self, instantly. So rather than question Himself, He questioned others, did He not?* [Chuckles]

For He indeed was helping to stimulate through the questioning, the realities of what they did not know, so they could open their pineal and know.

Kevin: Did any of His disciples have their pineal glands activated and opened?

Malachi: *That one which was called Mark. Disciple Mark did have the pineal open. Not in the beginning. It took some time of himself, and time after what was called the Transfiguration.*

[**Author's Note:** This occurred after the crucifixion. We will explain that in detail in the book *Jesus, the Prince of Peace.*]

Kevin: Did Mark travel with Jesus? To possibly, India? Kashmir?

Malachi: *Indeed, indeed. And he traveled with great faith. And in the faith, beautiful one, is what we call the knowing, and with that he worked diligently to release the juice of his body's brain. But it was receiving nothing but the Light, do you understand?*

Kevin: I feel little cracks, noises in the center of my head. Is that the calcification around my pineal gland? It is breaking up?

Malachi: *Indeed, indeed, indeed. That is you, allowing yourself to let the pineal gland shed its shield, the shield of protection. It is doing so in its increments, so again, that you do not have overwhelm. Do you understand?*

Kevin: My body, my matrix, could not handle such a large surge of energy all at once—if it opened up all at once?

Malachi: *Indeed, indeed, that is correct. You will notice that as this cracking is taking form, you will eventually feel what is called cellular vibrations all through the body, not simply the brain.*

You'll have, at times, the feeling that you need to look at your arm to make sure it's an arm. [Laughs] *Or another part of your body, to make sure it's a part of the body. That is because the vibrations of the physical are changing. And that which you called your natural self can no longer be the natural self. Because now you are shape-shifting to the more natural self.* [Laughs]

I am experiencing this even now, as I write this. It sometimes feels as if the top and back of my head are not solid, and are blending into the air or the field of energy around me. I am getting used to these sensations, just as I have become accustomed to the vibrational pressure that Saint Germain uses to show me that he is with me. It is strongly present now, as I write this.

Malachi: *So chemistries are taking place throughout the body. That is helping to change the body's frequencies for a higher vibration, or a more refined vibration. "Refined" meaning, you're coming more and more into the blend[ing] of your Divine Self in the human body.*

From Session L46 on 9.26.12 – Our Awareness of the New Earth – Messages from the Holy Mother and the Holy Father, Saint Germain (Saint Joseph)

Malachi: *Now, the Holy Mother in Her presence with you, is telling you this: In the human design, the human mind, and the human heart, there is this emergence. Here we have called it the Christed Being, have we not?*

She says unto yourselves, it is as though in your minds and in your awareness, there is a presentation of a baby child. What does that mean? Well, it means, treat your consciousness, treat the consciousness of the collective field, as though a baby has been birthed. There is celebration in that, is there not?

Kevin and Marina: Yes.

Malachi: *There is a tender care in that as well. And that is what She is asking—[for] the tender care of the birth of the new life that is fully blossoming, fully growing in the present now.*

But it is tenuous. Why is it tenuous? Well, you have but to look at your human condition and see why it is tenuous, do you not?

Humanity is still wanting to fight humanity. Humanity is still wanting to struggle with themselves. So She says to you [that] She comes here in your presence because of the sacred mind [and] sacred hearts that you are living in, [because of] your intention to help hold the Light in its higher power.

So we say to you, receive this energy, as though you are receiving a baby that you will nurture, you will hold sacred. You will encourage the loving Light to move beyond you and into this called your humanity, so that their hearts can maintain this loving Light as well, and be more receptive unto the new changes in the New World.

That is Her blessing to you. Saint Germain, we say, come forward Saint Germain. What would you care to share with these peoples? And his answer first is, I am sharing all the time!

Kevin: Yes. [Marina and Kevin laugh]

Malachi: *So, we will acknowledge that first and foremost, will we not. Now, he said this to you before, to take your walk in Nature. He repeats that very often, does he not?*

Kevin and Marina: Yes.

Malachi: *Now we will ask you, well—let that be the question. When you are walking, what are you receiving from Saint Germain?*

Kevin: I believe he is trying to get us to feel the energy coming from Mother Earth.

Marina: To be more connective to Mother Earth.

Malachi: *Indeed, indeed.*

Marina: To let our consciousness be more connected, rather than staying in our ego mind. And to actually feel Saint Germain, and maybe to talk to him more, and receive messages from him.

Malachi: *Indeed, indeed. And yes, he is asking you: With your feet, feel the essence of the Earth Mother, the consciousness of the Earth vibration-planet itself, changing.*

We have already shared with you [that] there are chakra center vortices that have taken up these beautiful shimmering lights. Allow yourself to feel that in the beautiful core of Earth. And when you can, when you connect, then allow yourselves, as though you are walking on a path, to follow the rays of Light, around the core of your Earth.

Why would you be asked to do that? He says unto you this: Every time you step into a frequency, a ray of Light, with the sacred heart, the sacred intention of your consciousness, you are helping increase it, not only to the Earth Mother Herself, but to your humanity.

It is time that the greater rays be taken up by all human beings meaning to utilize it. It is contained within them already, but very similar to what you have watched in the struggle of humans before, they may lock it in their unconscious, rather than releasing it.

He says to you: When you are walking upon the land and you are feeling the beauty of the vibrations of the inner core of Earth creating the ray changes throughout the Earth and the Earth people, when you are walking with such intentions of Divine Love, sacred attitude of recognizing [that] the great changes are for your Earth, for your Earth people, and the Earth conditions, you are helping to enhance the vibration of what is termed in your world as the Unconditional Love of the Universe.

And indeed, it merges into all conscious states of the beings that inhabit the Earth. So that is not only humans, is it, beautiful ones? It is the essence of all things that inhabit the Earth.

The beauty of your animal world, many species in great change, allowing that which is called the rays of Light to help change the configuration of matter, and it will affect human beings. Same for the plants, same for the minerals. But your animals are the closest connection to yourselves, do you understand? And so, here we are going to ask you to pay attention to the animals.

Now, you may pay attention to them through their Spirit, or your eyes can be wide open to pay attention to the birds in flight, those who crawl, and those who run on four feet, paying attention to all of it, do you understand?

And when you are seeing one, allow yourselves to blend. As we have been asking you to blend with Jesus, blend with the animal. Feel its Spirit. Notice, notice its beautiful expression of change. Now here, take a breath. [Pause]

Saint Germain asks of you in this very moment, to feel the vibration of the beautiful animals across your world. To feel how they are taking up the rays of Light themselves, and to feel the intentions they are carrying. I remind you here [that] the animals are that vibrational energy that is called "instinct." Instinct is a natural form in human beings as well, that reminds you how to care for yourselves.

We will ask you to feel how the animals are radiating an instinct of harmony between what is called the ethereal vibrations and the Earthly vibrations. If you will allow yourselves to blend into this, Saint Germain tells you, you will also sense what is called the change in the instinctual nature of humans.

So we will become quiet for a few moments, and allow you to feel that, and then you may offer what you recognize. [Pauses]

What are you noticing?

Kevin: I'm noticing something that humans don't generally notice, and that is no-time. I'm finding that the animals exist more in a no-time consciousness, from their instincts.

Malachi: *Very good. How do you recognize this helps? How can this help your humanity?*

Kevin: Well, it definitely eliminates stress. It eliminates what controls humanity, because time controls humanity.

Malachi: *Indeed, indeed. That is a very important notice, is it not? Now, how can you write about that, beautiful one? You see, Saint Germain desires [that] you continue to write the knowledge. Notice what you have felt, and write about it.*

Humanity wants to find their clocks, do they not? Humanity wants to be on their schedules. The animals do not. They move through natural rhythm, and that is what is called unto humanity, "Move with natural rhythm. You will always be on time." [Kevin laughs]

Anything else you wish to share about this beautiful realm called the Spirit of the Animals?

Marina: I just felt more connected to animals, and I felt that I have so much more respect for them too, because we are living on the same planet. They are part of me, as I am part of them.

Malachi: *Indeed.*

Marina: And it just feels good to have that Love and respect for them. I wish more people would have that.

Malachi: *Then we shall invite you again. The more you feel it, the more you recognize it, the more respect you carry for these beautiful Spirits of Nature, the more you will propagate that vibration to the collective consciousness.*

And it can be felt you see, beautiful one, even if only one of you [does this]. [It] can make quite an effect to the collective. Why? Because it is the power of your Peacefulness, the power of your harmony, and the power of your Love.

It penetrates the field, and the field begins to take notice. So we will call it simply the field of the collective conscious[ness] of humanity. While you have been sitting here, Saint Germain wishes you to know [that] you have been affecting the collective field of humanity by noticing the spirit of the animals. He says to you, will you give at least five minutes a day for that experience to occur?

Kevin: Yes, we will.

Malachi: *A simple five minutes, that is all that is required here, to create a vibration that waves through the collective field, do you understand? You may choose to have several five minutes of the day.*

All right, we will see if he wishes to ask for you more. Indeed, he does. All right, beautiful ones. He brings forward a sunrise. Do you enjoy sunrise?

Marina: Yes, it's beautiful.

Kevin: I do it when it's not cloudy. I'm outside every morning.

Malachi: *Indeed, indeed*

Kevin: On nice sunny days.

Malachi: *In that will you know this, to yourselves—the sun rises in your East, does it not? It is the place of the great Masters. And so, as you notice your sunrise, as you notice that envelope of energy called sunrise, would you also allow yourselves the acknowledgement of the blend[ing] with the Masters.*

For each of your day as you are doing that, the blend[ing] with the Masters allows a conscious exchange from the Masters, to you and from you to them, in which you can be guided. Guided for your day's work, your day's interaction, and opportunities for you. To know what it is you can do, to help with this collective field continue to rise in their Light. Do you understand?

Marina: Yes.

Malachi: *Back we go to the Mother Earth, he says. Back we go to the Mother Earth. All right. Re-enter the beautiful core of the Mother Earth. Feel Her rhythm. Feel Her rhythm as She is taking up the rays of Light, as She is allowing the new emergence of consciousness. And again, we shall come quiet, so you may feel, hear and be inspired.* [Pauses for several minutes]

And again we will ask you, what do you notice?

Kevin: What I notice is happiness. I see and feel a happy energy there, in the core of the Earth. You could say, it is the image of the Source, Peace and harmony, Love and happiness, and almost an innocence. But also the knowledge of knowing what's on the surface sometimes. I see the sending of rays to the surface that try to bring Love and Light to the Earth's surface.

Malachi: *Indeed.*

Kevin: And I feel that the core of the Earth is not really alone, even though a lot of humans are not in unison with the fullness of the Mother Earth's presence. I do feel that the mineral kingdom around it is.

Malachi: *Indeed. Would you also feel the animal kingdom?*

Kevin: I was thinking that.

Malachi: *You see here, your animal, plant and mineral more easily align with the natural energy fields, which take form from the very core of the Earth, to that which you call the crust of the Earth. And from there, presented to humanity so you recognize, it is through these elements that there is a sustaining to you.*

So, as we have shared before, these sustain you. You must sustain them. How do you do it? How do you help sustain the Earth Mother, in order to sustain the mineral, the plant, and the animals?

Kevin: We give Her our Love and Light.

Malachi: *Indeed, Indeed. And you listen, and you listen well, you feel, and you feel the depth of the wisdom that merges through you, then you respond. To respond means that if you feel the need to take an action, you take the action, do you not? If you feel the need to simply relax, blend and be, that's all you do.*

Above all, you maintain the reality that there is nothing wrong, that everything is moving in its Divine right plan, and yes, its Divine right timing. The Earth consciousness is [experiencing] a grand, grand and delightful change. So worry not. Simply be with it.

Kevin: OK.

Malachi: *All right—next question!*

Kevin: Can you say that the Earth has already ascended?

Malachi: *Indeed. Indeed it has.*

Kevin: The June 5, 2012 Venus Transit—was that a particular date when the Earth ascended, or somewhere around that date?

Malachi: *Well, beautiful one, you may say, throughout this given time frame. So we will call it a circle of time of your 2012 [that] has allowed all of this to occur.*

Now we have shared with you that the coming of December [2012] is the full-on anchoring, as it will be played out for centuries to come. Do you understand?

Kevin: Yes.

Malachi: *So are we not calling all of humanity to align in such a center point of Peace, [so] that [Peace] is will be completely anchored? That these Light rays that have already formulated the ascension, that has already occurred, [that] every human being can blend with such ascension, and realize it within themselves, and call themselves to the Peacefulness that Earth Mother radiates, [which] the great Divine Source has already impregnated in itself, called matter. And all of the animal, plant, minerals and even your humanness, you are already the Light.*

Well, take it up, because in the human design, you have the configuration of the choice power. And the choice power can leave you either believing you are "less than" or that you are Divine. That is what you are learning, are you not?

And that is what you are willing to take up, within your hearts and minds. Hold it steady—yes, as you are being asked, because when you do, that is what you are radiating throughout your Earth. Your Earth peoples, the collective field, they gather it.

From Session L32 on 1.31.13 – Honoring the Divine Feminine

Malachi: *Indeed, very good, very good. Quan Yin is here on this day.*

Marina: Greetings, Quan Yin.

Malachi: *And as She does step forward, She does indeed make this acknowledgement. Will you allow yourselves, for the next three days, to be in the power of devotion to the holy feminine, to the Divine Mother, that you will unify and feel yourselves unifying with that Divine Feminine consciousness?*

And She tells you why: Once again, the feminine principal of the consciousness used by humanity moves the energy of nurturing and compassion to a more refined level. You already know that the Divine Feminine principle of consciousness being used, is the awareness that there has been a birth of the New World.

And in this timing frame that She is asking for you to honor or pay attention to, it's a timing frame in which a celebration to the Divine, to the feminine principal of consciousness, gives honor to this birth and to its growth, again its cultivation. Indeed, She is also working right along with Saint Germain, and saying, "Here, listen to us, and we will speak about the devotion to the Feminine." And so, again another layer of your writing, is it not?

Kevin: Yes.

Malachi: *We are watching Her, as She frames Her energy in a glow of pure white Light, with the glittering of the gold. Now,*

beautiful ones, you know the glittering of the gold, do you not?

Here we have been honoring, through the beautiful, shimmering, pearlized Light, the shimmering gold in the ninth chakra. The vibration chakra that brings the cosmic rhythm and the Earthly rhythm into unification, and the higher causal energies for developing this New World, can be felt in a rhythm.

So She says to you: For the next few days—three—here will you allow yourselves to find a rhythm in your step, a rhythm in your words, that you will use as though a prayer or a mantra. Create this as your centering point within you, to call forward in the sacred matrix of your whole being that Divine Feminine wisdom that is being processed, and does indeed need words.

Marina and I did write short rhythmic songs that we sang while moving our bodies in rhythmic steps. We did this for three days, and encourage everyone to do this.

This world began with the word of Wisdom, the Holy Spirit. Now She is asking for your words to assist in bringing Her beautiful Essence to the forefront during the birth of our New World.

Notice that Malachi and Quan Yin are speaking about the ninth chakra. We are presently working on a book which speaks about the new chakra system for humans and for the Earth, titled *The New Human Template for a New World.*

Chapter Ten

The Birth of the Christ Within Us

The Prince of Peace, the Christed Self within all, has come out of the darkness and into the Light of my being and my awareness.

~ Malachi

From Session L1 on 12.19.12:

Malachi: *All right, beautiful ones, as we enter, do you feel us surround you?*

Kevin and Marina: Yes. Yes we do.

Malachi: *Do you feel the Love blessings?*

Marina and Kevin: Yes, we do, thank you. Thank you.

Malachi: *Indeed, they are there constantly, and yet when we enter this body-mind consciousness to share with you on the tonality of your Earth plane, there is a burst of Light energy that we present, and you did indeed receive it already. And so again we say, greetings and blessings!*

Marina: Greetings.

Malachi: *Indeed, and beautiful ones, we always say, take a deep breath, do we do not.*

[Marina and Kevin breathe deeply]

Malachi: *And we will ask of you, to do that that you feel in your breath, the centering of your consciousness, and the beauty that you can feel in your holy inner temple.*

For you are igniting Light in your holy inner temple that does indeed radiate. Radiate through your earth realm unit of consciousness, as well as the multi–dimensions. And so every time you breathe with such an awareness, you are increasing that Light vibration. Did you know this?

Kevin: I didn't think about it in that way, but it makes perfect sense as you say it.

Malachi: *Indeed. All right, you have received blessings of Light, you are extending blessings of Light, that which you call the murmurs of the White Brotherhood all around you, and around your great Earth.*

You now have an awareness of why we have been calling for the Peace, do you not? A greater awareness of why we have been asking you to shed Light?

Kevin: Yes.

Malachi: *Now, beautiful ones, take another breath, and shed that Light again, that there is what is called the vibrational energies and activations of greater Peace in the hearts of humanity, and most particularly, your nation, that comes across the world again, to all other nations, calling on the power of Peace and the beauty of the harmony.*

Here, here again, the great One that taught all of you how to come to your Christed self, Jesus, Yahweh, Yeshua—all names that you wish to call this Being—is present.

And yes, Saint Germain is present, and yes, Jared, who has asked us to acknowledge his presence. So we will acknowledge that, will we not?

As Jesus steps forwards, He wishes to make acknowledgements for you, as to what you have received as you have walked through the year called 20 and 12. For you received an opening in your consciousness, did you not?

You received the greater awareness of the ability of thought and emotional vibrations of Love, channeling through yourselves Union, as you call it, with the Divine Mind and its units of consciousness, called the master-verse. And so He is acknowledging that to you.

You have opened your channel. You have been blessed by the Divine to have this opening within you. And there shall be continuance of this expansion of your consciousness and your communication with the Divine levels, multi-dimensions and Beings. It has been strongly imprinted in your consciousness throughout your 20 and 12. It will indeed merge right on in with intention through your 20 and 13.

Here this Divine One [Jesus] wishes also to tell you what you have imprinted to the world. For as you have received, you have acted upon what you have received, and you have been sending blessing vibrations to create Peace and harmony in your Earth unit, and you have reflected it back unto the beautiful Divine.

From yourselves, you are showing the Divine that you have been learning how to be still in your mind and emotional consciousness, in order to receive inspiration, and in order then to send it forth unto the world, called your human unit, the Earth unit of consciousness.

At times, He says of you, you would feel your anxiousness of receiving messages and inspiration. Yet that has already changed within you—the anxiousness [is] quelling, is it not?

Kevin: Yes, it is.

Malachi: *Here He honors also, that you have created a stronger commitment to follow the path of Spirit, the higher nature of yourselves, the beautiful nature of Oneness.*

As you are doing that, you are indeed leaving an imprint to your humanity to be able to follow. And we know we have shared this before, yet again, we wish to claim it with you, that you have such realization of what has occurred already in your 20 and 12 and to prepare the way for you for your 20 and 13.

Here the Christed One does say to you, the heavenly energies will continue to imprint within you your awareness of Union in Divine consciousness. It will continue to imprint within your personality the awareness of how to communicate with the Masters, with the awareness of how to communicate from your Divine Christed center, and indeed, out and through the world.

Indeed, as you continue to march through your next year, you will feel stronger and stronger impressions for the writings that you have been asked to do, and more that you will do. And as you will take this up again, do note you will be printing this knowledge for others to know.

You will also realize [that] what you are doing through these words is creating healings of consciousness. And Jesus does want you to know, that in these healings of consciousness, you will not only affect the adults that are willing to read and learn and explore, but you will be helping the wee ones, the children of the world. And this becomes most important, as they become the next Masters that teach, do they not?

You will find that you will have many choices, as your year opens up, for you to follow through with your intentions as healers, as teachers, as listeners to the great words of the Divine and of the living power of the One unit.

You of yourselves will also continue to leave your mark upon the Earth. He recognizes your sacred intentions and says yes, they will even grow stronger in mystical wisdom, in gathering of the knowledge, and will begin imprinting stronger awareness to your brothers and sisters of humanity, of how to live Oneness, how to speak Oneness, how to harmonize in the Oneness, and how to live your Christed self. That will continue in its growth in your next year called 20 and 13.

Kevin: Great.

Marina: Wonderful. Exciting!

Malachi: *All right, take a breath again, and feel those blessings penetrate yourselves. Right, beautiful ones, do you wish to question this day?*

Marina: Would Saint Germain or Jared like to speak?

Malachi: *Saint Germain is in the present moment standing behind you, dear woman. As he does, we are going to ask you to feel the energy that he moves down your back muscles. Can you feel it?*

Marina: Yes, I do feel it.

Malachi: *The vibration of this is [a] gentle motion, to relax the muscles of your body, [to] hold the body intention, and therefore are very receptive to energy fields that bring you balance—indeed, bring Love vibrations, and continue to bring healing vibrations through your body.*

Marina: Thank you.

Malachi: [Laughs] *Saint Germain says this to the both of you: In your next week ahead of yourselves, will you present yourselves with what is called completions, so [that] you look around your busyness and you will ask yourselves, What is it that I can complete, where I can be in the sacredness of transition? Transitions, beautiful ones, we have been calling them transformations, have we not?*

Well, this is termed transition. But it is not about how the human consciousness must have its great transformation, but the transition of its Light. The transition of its higher intentions, and therefore, Saint Germain is saying, make way, that nothing be sitting about yourselves that you would say is your busyness. That nothing be sitting about yourselves, that you will be called into attention to do something about, until after what is termed to yourselves that the brilliance of the Light frequencies of intentions, into what is called your New Year. Are you able to do this, beautiful ones?

Kevin: Yes, we will definitely focus on this and finish up anything that is "open" and unfinished.

Marina: Thank you.

Malachi: *Indeed, indeed. Yes, beautiful ones, we are going to say this to you. More Light frequencies increasing the higher consciousness of the New World are occurring, [and] will continue to occur as you enter your 12 and 21 day* [12/21/12]. *And so, you asked to be receptive to it, are you not?*

Kevin: Yes.

Malachi: *And after you have been receptive to it, to indeed use the power of the silence. So allow yourselves on such a day to enter times of silence. It does not have to be your entire day or two or three days. Yet find times that you are having nothing but silence for a stretch of your time. Two or three hours of your time, where you are but nothing except receptive, nothing but receptive, that your minds do not travel to what might be occurring or how it may manifest itself in your future.*

Let your heart simply be the vehicle of Love and the vehicle of reception that allows you to feel the blessings that are occurring. Then, beautiful ones, once you have allowed this time and space to occur for you, then will you bring out what is termed in the darkness of part of your evening time, the beauty of candles. Why?

Because then you see the flame of Spirit, the Light of higher intention. And as you allow yourselves to light your candles, you are coming out of darkness, and you may say an affirmative prayer:

> The Prince of Peace, the Christed Self within all, has come out of the darkness and into the Light of my being and my awareness.
>
> This Light I radiate. It is the Light of Peace. It is the Light of Love. It is the I Am Presence seen, felt, known. I AM the Light. I AM the Light. I AM the Light.

Then you are asked to sit with these flames of awareness, feeling your affirmative statements, knowing you have lifted the Christed Light within yourselves to be seen.

Indeed, beautiful ones, it is a sacred act to bring this Light, this frequency of awareness to the forefront of your being, and it does indeed create a very positive energy effect throughout your world.

[Laughs] *I have a good giggle for you: Jared is moving all about yourselves as though he were a tidy bug.* [All laugh] *And he will work with you, to tidy up the air, to fruition.*

Marina: Thank you, Jared.

Malachi: *And periodically, you feel as though there is urgency. Well, that is Jared, for he will be urgently helping. Desirous and joyful, in the helping mood. We shall call him Tidy Bug for a while, shall we do that?* [All laugh]

Even unto his spirit, he places the laughter with you, for it is of his desire to be so personal, that he can help you with such energy fields. Do you understand?

Kevin and Marina: Thank you, Jared.

Malachi: *Now, beautiful ones, let's have you take another breath. We shall honor again the beauty of the Masters that are with you. We call ourselves a group, do we not? A conscious state.*

It is a conscious state of mercy, of Love. It is a conscious state of healing, so you can call yourselves in that regard consciously, mercifully relating to all people with the healing vibration, through the Light of Love. To spread that vibration, to continue to spread that vibration, to offer that vibration at any time.

The thought field wanders about your Earth people. You create a wave of energy that helps all come to their center point. Can you allow yourselves to feel the encircled vibration around your Earth, by the beautiful ones that are called the White Brotherhood, by the beautiful ones that are called the Angels of Mercy, and by the beautiful ones that are called the Archangels of consciousness?

All [are] part of the great net of the universe, revealing their individual unit into the world. They do this at times stronger than other times. Why? Well, at times it is because of the human collective field, and indeed, beautiful ones, what has been occurring across your Earth, as we called you into Peaceful prayerful harmonies to move across your Earth, as Quan Yin did share with you, as we have all shared with you, [to] help to hold the network of harmony.

And disasters seem to run, traumas seem to run onto the pathway of Earth's people. And so the strengthening of these calls for help has the strengthening for each of you to feel and to sense this beautiful encompassing of Light and Love, Healing and Peace.

There is another reason why they are so strong in the here and now, and it is because of this great transition. It is because these beings of consciousness are celebrating the new states, the entry of the vibrations into the Earth plane, sealing the energies. Sealing the energies, for future generations. This is also a time in the consciousness that hears your call [to the] collective field of humans, that have identified this time as celebration times through religious belief systems.

And whenever you have such strengths in the call to celebrations such as this, the collective field of the human unit calls on all of the higher fields to be more prevalent, to be felt more strongly.

And so you have this experience, where you can sense and feel around the field of your Earth plane, the glory of these Divine essences of the unit of the Divine expression. Can you feel yourselves as part of this grouping of consciousness?

Kevin and Marina: I can. Yes.

Malachi: *Do you realize that not only can you feel yourselves on the Earth, but in the aura of the Earth, radiating with the grand Masters?*

Kevin: Yes.

Malachi: *Very good, very good. Now, beautiful ones, we shall also acknowledge this reality. Here you can say [that] there are thousands and thousands of human beings that are walking with the intention to live a Master consciousness, so many that indeed are allowing the acceptance through the collective field of the New World. So many, indeed, that this is now weaving this imagery of the fifth-dimensional world into a strengthened position of human consciousness.*

Indeed, this allows what is also termed "the thinning of the veils" of the realms of consciousness, the dimensions. And again, feel the celebration of the ethereal brothers and sisters, the galactic brothers and sisters. The dimensional consciousness says that you can call singular units in the infinite net of the grand design, celebrating.

We shall share with you again, that in such vibrational exchanges, this will open the doorways of human design, human consciousness, to be more receptive. Not only to inspiration, but to the living matter beyond your human field. Your scientists [will be] more receptive, being able to open the portals of communication with galactic beings. More studies will increase.

Shall we say, beautiful ones, this is a time when there will be an end to the silence between the dimensions, a time that is heralding the end of silence between the galactic brothers and sisters and the human brothers and sisters.

You will again be aware—be alert, as we call it—over your

Earthly time, as to how this develops. We speak this to yourselves, because you know of the existence of other beings.

This also means, to yourselves, the portals are open. The doorways are open. The veil is thinner—however you want to name it. Yourselves, in this grand [Earth] unit, will have more awareness of the galactic beings communicating with you.

Marina: Can they come and visit?

Malachi: *If you will invite them, they will. All right, now take another breath. We are being told by Saint Germain to also acknowledge to you that you are going to be paying attention to a greater sensitivity of your fields of energy.*

Now, let us explain this to you. It is not simply an intuitive sensitivity. It is energetic sensitivity. And what this means to yourselves, is that your own skins will seem to have a greater awareness of energies charging into your aura, and into your physicality. At times, it may feel like you must scratch your body because of the energy. Have you already begun to feel this?

Kevin: I think so. I was scratching right before you said it. [All laugh]

Malachi: *This is your sensitivity to the vibrational energies that the human consciousness, before now, before the lifting of the veils, was not sensitive [to], in awareness as to what was occurring, therefore nullifying any of the energy being sent, shared or explored.*

Yourselves, with your higher intentions being indeed activated, is allowing yourselves to lift those veils around you in the human field of energy, so that you can indeed experience much more than the dimensional vibrations.

And yes, it will mean that there is almost an irritant to the skin. But that is simply because the human quality of skin consciousness must get used to the new frequencies being felt, so you will notice how at times it is almost an irritant. At times, it is simply a need to have a scratch on the body, and as you are doing so, give a blessing to it making an acknowledgement: "I am aware of the changes of vibration."

This is what you can say in acknowledgement, "I am aware." This helps your unconscious mind be more receptive to the energy fields. All right. Has this imposed questions in your consciousness now?

Kevin: I'm just trying to absorb everything. We talked about the 21st [of December 2012]. So I am not really asking any questions, because you basically asked us not to have any expectations.

Malachi: *Indeed, Indeed.*

Kevin: So that takes away the ability to ask questions!

Malachi: *It does indeed, does it not? We continue to tell you to be receptive. Receptive to the vibrations, to the thought-forms, to the experiences. Indeed, yes, indeed. And that leaves you as vehicles, vessels, chalices, receiving and receiving and receiving.*

Kevin: On that day, what you are asking us to do, is to create a time period of about three hours when we are in total silence, and are attentive to the silence as well?

Malachi: *Indeed.*

Kevin: Without any expectation of what is going on around us, what may happen, or what we might feel—just to be receptive?

Malachi: *Just to be receptive, that is correct.*

Kevin: OK. Very good.

Malachi: *Beautiful ones, if your minds want to run into activity, then we would suggest that you do several things to help the receptive nature, to utilize different senses of yourself.*

So [for] the sense of hearing, you can put the sounds of soft music. To the sense of smell, you can place what is called sacred aromas. Do you understand? That will help you be more receptive to the silent points of yourself. Inner qualities of yourself.

To the power of touch, beautiful ones, you can bring what is called the sacred stone into your hands. To help your conscious mind remember, stay focused only on the sacred receptive energy. Feel of yourself. So there you have what is called hearing, smelling and touching, do you not?

Marina: Yes.

Kevin: Would that be a clear crystal stone? Would that be best?

Malachi: *Very good, a clear crystal stone would be very good. And then you balance into your silent point. And before long you will not hear if you have music playing, and you will not smell your aromas, nor will you feel your stone.*

For you will have entered the pure point of receptivity, which is near the point of No Thing. Then you can allow yourselves to be in such position for a very long period of time on your Earth timing clock.

Kevin: What happens if we fall asleep?

Malachi: *Very good. Then your conscious mind would have quieted, would it not? And your subconscious mind will be the active energy, remaining very receptive to the fields of consciousness, the blessings of Light that you will be receiving.*

Kevin: So it matters not?

Malachi: *Matters not that you fall asleep. Be in the peaceful comfort, and allow.*

Kevin: Does the time matter, on December 21st? Could it be done very early in the morning, or afternoon? I know you talked about using the candles in the evening. Is this to be separate?

Malachi: *You can allow it to be two separate events. And you are correct, [the time of] it does not matter, beautiful ones. For in the scheme of time energy, that is human, time energy, is it not?*

And so you say, it is by intention of the day. And so if you chose to have your silence in your morning, you're fine. In your afternoon, you're fine. In your night, you're fine. It is the power of the intention. For the radiance, it will be there, it is there, it is increasing and it will increase throughout what is termed your day of December 21. You will not leave [the Earth] after that day. [All laugh]

It is simply waves that will be called increased energy fields, strengthened energy fields, as it were. So yes, beautiful ones, power of intention. That is what you will use. Power of intention. And we will honor that again in this fashion, the power of intention. Shall [even if] you fall asleep, you have already set the intention, have you not?

Kevin: Yes.

Malachi: *So it merges with your human consciousness. It serves in your human endeavors to assist you to receive these waves, without expectation. Yes, without judgment. Yes, without dictating how we want [it]. All aspects of yourself will be set to be receptive by your intentions. Do you have another question now?*

Kevin: Yes. We haven't worked with our son, Vaju Entlis, in quite a while. What shall we ask him to be doing on the 21st?

Malachi: *You may also ask of him to take some time of quiet. You most certainly can ask of him to participate with you, to acknowledging the Light frequency with the candles.*

You can indeed share with him that this is a very special time that is opening the gateways, the gateways of the human consciousness, to the multi, multi-regions of the grand Universal Mind.

You can allow him to know, that this is a time where the gateways are open between humanity and the galactic beings, and to call on those galactic beings that serve in the highest levels of Divine consciousness.

This is what you can ask of your son. [Laughing] *You might ask him to be tidying, with Jared!* [All laugh] *Let him know that we are calling Jared "the tidy bug." Perhaps he will be able to feel Jared's energy—precise, swift movement. Does this help you?*

Kevin: Yes, it does very much, thank you. And what about other people whom we know and talk to? If they ask us what we recommend, or what they should be doing or thinking? Because I don't know what to tell them.

Malachi: *Indeed. Well, beautiful ones, share with them what your intentions are, what your focus will be. Ask them to align, simply meaning, to come into the silence, to be receptive to sacred inspiration, sacred energies, and sacred direction.*

Remind them to be receptive beings, that they do not try to configure or expect, but to be receptors, allowing energy to pass through them. Remind them to be open in their hearts, which means to all of you, to be heartfelt with Love, Compassion and Peace.

You may encourage them to utilize the candles and let the Light emerge in their conscious awareness. And, beautiful ones, as you allow yourselves to set your day's frequency and your night's frequency, remind yourselves that you are allowing your intentions to be waves of consciousness, the move to the collective field in the unit of humanity.

And so know that you will be encouraging others [that] you do not even speak with, others humanly you do not even know, to perform the rite of awareness, the rite of Light, the rite of Love. Indeed, does this also help you?

Kevin: Yes, very much.

Malachi: *All right. Another question?*

Kevin: It seems like most people are just going to go about their day, like it's just another day.

Malachi: *Indeed.*

Kevin: And then there are a few people that are feeling fearful, because of what the media has put out about this time, which is wrong. I don't think too many people feel fearful about it, but some people do.

Malachi: *Indeed, that is correct. Some do. Some do, but beautiful ones, you are correct. There are many people that will simply go about their business, having no thought, no intention, and no awareness.*

There are also thousands of you that come to this time, this day, this event, with an awareness, an intention. And you are servants of all. Serving the power of such Light. Anchoring the vibrations, the seeds of the New World, looming from your intentions.

We [will] have a bit of a philosophy with you. We [will] have you think more philosophically—that's your word?—philosophically, all right. The beauty of the nature of the Oneness has been cultivating this New Garden, and has been seeding it, developing the seeds of the new state of consciousness. Your intentions have indeed assisted in germinating the seeds, so they can burst forth from the soil of the deeper unconscious.

Please know that, imagine that, feel it, and recognize [that] the seeds are germinated. They are bursting forth. You, your family, you have carried an intention to be able to support the consciousness of the sacred reality.

Note how many thousands of other people are doing the very same thing, carrying such an intention. Note this as well, for you read of those who have been following the White Brotherhood for years. You call it years, and we shall say, for hundreds of years, all of them helping to prepare the way, and the way of this timing is now.

The timing is bursting forth. Yes, it is well known to your consciousness, those of you who are searching the Wisdom, that an era or eon completes itself about every 26,000 years. And that means a new eon and a new era is ready to burst from the seeds in the New Garden.

You will have helped germinate them, and you are helping

to cultivate the life force of this New World generation of consciousness.

Now, will you allow yourselves to confirm and offer to return to the era of Light, return to the era of Peace, return to the era of Compassion?

And we give honor back unto you, that we know as you have taken up this commitment, that you will cultivate your lives in such a manner that you will feel the harmony of it, even when you may see your brothers and sisters of humanity that are choosing to remain in ignorance, until the strengthened life force or we will call it, the plants of the Garden, are so strongly developed, that they cannot be ignored. Do you comprehend this?

Kevin: Yes, very much.

Malachi: *Very good. Take another breath. We will remind you that you are given honor this day, for how you have allowed yourselves to open the channel of consciousness throughout this year, that in turn you have indeed been radiating Lights, Lights that do indeed reflect upon your world—how to come to the center point, come into the harmony, the Peace radiated.*

We shall laugh with you, and say "be prepared," for the inspiration will become stronger again, and stronger again, and you will, must indeed, commit it to paper. Writing the words, giving your guidance—will you do that?

Kevin: Yes, very much. We will do that.

Malachi: *Indeed. All right, beautiful ones, do you have another question or are you complete on this day?*

Kevin and Marina: We are complete. Thank you, Malachi.

Chapter Eleven

Mother Mary Leads Us to Receive Her Holy Spirit

> *Let the circuitry of Light pass through you. Let the circuitry of Light infiltrate the field of human reality.*
>
> ~ Mother Mary, the Holy Spirit

From Session L84 on 8.8.13:

Malachi: *All right, beautiful ones. We enter into your realm. And indeed, we ask of you to take the breath, to feel the presence, to feel the presence of the Masters with you, to feel the presence of the Masters within you.*

And as you do, your breathing becomes a synchronicity. You're not only breathing with the presence, you're breathing with its individual qualities—as we would call it, the White Brotherhood—in this moment. Yet we would ask you to feel in your breathing how you are indeed a part of the Whole.

Now let us have you both breathe again. And breathe the joy of your journey, for you have been taking quite a journey here, have you not?

Kevin and Marina: Yes.

Malachi: *Are there questions?*

Kevin: Yesterday, I brought up about speaking to the Holy Spirit in the body.

Malachi: *Indeed.*

Kevin: Are we going to do that today?

Malachi: *You are indeed!* [All laugh]

We will first invite you to allow your consciousness to make [the] ascension vibration occur—to take your deep breath again, [and] to feel the glory of all who are working with you, the Masters.

And as you do, may we ask you to feel that vibration of ascending consciousness, and enter into the Sacred Temple. [Pause] *Be embraced by the energy of Love, the beauty of the Light in the temple, the graciousness of the Spirit Ones, the White Brotherhood.*

[Silence]

In this temple, feel the presence rise within yourselves, the presence rise, of the Holy Spirit.

[Silence]

Mary, the Holy Spirit: *In your presence I AM.*

Kevin and Marina: Greetings, Holy Spirit.

Mary, the Holy Spirit: *As you are taking on a blessing, do not be disturbed by the pressure in your brain. The blessing of Light penetrating your brain, your pineal gland, must pass through great density, the material essence of your body. Relax in sacred repose, for then you take on the blessing with the ease that illuminates your being.*

Interlock your thumbs, your middle finger, and your smallest finger. Bring them together. Bring your largest toe of your right and left foot together. You are forming a circuit in Light frequency that is allowing the healing energy, the Light energy to move through every essence of your being. Now bring your middle fingers to the thumb, and hold that pose.

As you allow yourself to feel this frequency, acknowledge the affirming statement, I Am . . .

Kevin and Marina: I Am . . .

Mary, the Holy Spirit: *I Am the circuitry of the Holy Spirit.*

Kevin and Marina: I Am the circuitry of the Holy Spirit.

Mary, the Holy Spirit: *Allow yourselves such a statement. I Am the circuitry of the Holy Spirit.*

Kevin and Marina: I Am the circuitry of the Holy Spirit.

Mary, the Holy Spirit: *Feel the warmth of Spirit rising within you. Feel the essence of the Holy Spirit in your Oneness. Feel the radiance grow stronger. Bring all fingers to thumb. Allow your hands to open. Let the circuitry of Light pass through you. Let the circuitry of Light infiltrate the field of human reality.*

[Silence]

Dear ones of the Holy Spirit, you have asked for my presence. I am here. Place a signature on your desires. Bring your desires toward. What do you desire of me?

Kevin: Thank you very much for that. I was wondering if you could tell us about your life—when you were born and incarnated as Mary, or Miriam, and about growing up as the Holy Spirit, in a physical body, in that lifetime?

Mary, the Holy Spirit: *Shall I begin with the desire?*

Kevin: Yes.

Mary, the Holy Spirit: *From the realm of non-matter, the desire was birthed to bring to the realm of matter, a loving existence. To reveal to cultures a loving power, to bend a presence of consciousness, to impress, as your world says, to the collective field, to impress a consciousness of Love. In the essence of separation, the human field had been more of what you call war, harm, separation.*

I entered the field to help the human field remember the power of Love, the graciousness of community. In community, when ones are sharing in the capacity of Love, there is more than just the sweetness of joy. There is a power of Peace. There is the vibration of health. There is the bringing forth within your community a freedom from diseases—diseases that harm the body, diseases that harm the mind, diseases that harm the heart.

Unto My world of matter, I explored the great experience of sadness, the depth of sorrow. I returned into matter the image of a Virgin Mother, that [human] ones could know a purity of mind, that ones could know the purity of heart, ones could know the purity of the body, and ones could know the purity of Spirit in matter. That humanity would realize this grace is of them, [is] within them, is them.

Not only was there a choice to live that, as an embodied

individual, but the choice to bring forth a body, that ones might see the beauty and the graciousness, the active power of the Holy Spirit.

And thus, upon the Earth, I translated an energy into matter. Left upon the Earth an imprint, a vibration, for all to follow, blend into, and be. A gift unto humanity, as though a structural design to follow.

Feel unto your heart the Holy Spirit. As you feel and recognize the Holy Spirit, what is the experience of your heart-mind being?

Kevin: I do feel a great Oneness, and a connection with all my being. And I feel that the ego mind, the lower ego mind, as I receive the Holy Spirit, is being turned off. It's almost put me to sleep too, in doing that, by just not thinking.

And my body feels the vibration. My head feels the vibration, a lot of vibration. So if I close my eyes, I feel myself vibrating, and I don't quite feel the perimeters of my body so exactly in this physical realm.

Mary, the Holy Spirit: *In that moment, [that] you are feeling of your body, you are feeling [it as] the container of the Holy Spirit. When your human mind desires to sleep in the Spirit, it is because you are feeling only Peace.*

In the design of the human mind is a design of activity. Of yourselves, you will recognize the mind design is busyness. Searching, researching, comprehending, realizing. In your moments of Peace, you are very vulnerable.

In the human experience, to feel vulnerability causes an alertness. For still, many humans are afraid of the vulnerability, and prefer the busy, researching mind. Yet in the design of every aspect of life is vulnerability, receptivity. Both fields of energy are necessary.

As you are vulnerable, receiving the stirrings within the personal self [as it] calls for many designs to occur, you have been learning a design of healing. Your hearts, your minds, your bodies, have been asked to be active, allowing the flow of your awareness to occur.

Yet you have been asked to be receptive, vulnerable, that an increase of a sacred awareness within you can occur, an increase in alignment with the health, the Love, the joy of all. That you might pass the energies through you, to help your brothers, your sisters, your animals, your plants, the wisdom of soul, also be receptive. [Pause] We shall leave you with that to contemplate.

Kevin: Thank you very much. That's great.

Marina: Thank you. Thank you.

Malachi: [Chuckles] *All right, beautiful beings. What do you know [that] you have learned this day?*

Kevin: That once we have received the Holy Spirit, and are aware of the Holy Spirit, we are separate from our ego. We are in the Oneness, which apparently we are not used to. [Malachi and Kevin laugh]

Malachi: *Indeed, indeed. You experience a difference in your frequency do you not?*

Kevin: Yes.

Marina: Yes, it's very strong. It put me almost to sleep.

Malachi: *Indeed. Now, beautiful ones, as we call you to breathe, to feel us, we'll call you to breathe, to be aware of the sensations in your cells filled with the essence, purity of awareness, of the Holy Spirit.*

We did hear the Holy Spirit tell you It leaves you at Peace. The human mind goes to sleep. It has nothing to work upon, for it is all that It is. [Chuckles] *Shall you have a very good giggle?*

Kevin: Yes.

Malachi: *This will help you understand why there are individual components, and why when you study the mysteries of the grand Universe, and you enter the greater stages of consciousness we call bliss, [that] it can put you to sleep, and the essence of the Divine sleeps and is awake through you.*

This is why we teach you who believe of yourselves, in separation, [to be] so unimportant, [that in fact] you're ***very*** *important. For without the components active, there would be a deep sleep occurring.*

The components active allow the Holy Spirit to fulfill the desire of the designs. In your reality, we shall say [that within] the designs of the Earth, your Milky Way galaxy, the designs of all that you of yourselves are experiencing, the designs of the dimensions to be recognized, felt and utilized—you are important. What do you recognize in these statements?

Kevin: That we are, I can use the word, representative of the Holy Spirit here on this Earth plane. So if we manage to stay in this Oneness realm, Oneness awareness, we can be a representative of Holy Spirit, the Agents of Light, as you have called it before, but in this Earthly realm.

By manifesting good, beautiful things, by healing. By touching the other kingdoms of the world—animal, plant, mineral—with Light and Love, and just creating a great world of Light and Love, by being the Presence, the I Am, the Holy Spirit.

Malachi: *Indeed. You are the joy of Being. You are the expression of Being. You are the verb "to be," are you not?*

Kevin: To be active.

Malachi: *The acting, that is correct. And so we say, you may take that as a very serious job, where you may delight in simply the expression of Being. The allowing of yourselves to recognize that every thought, every emotion, every action, every interaction, is a beautiful Being state.*

As we ask of you to look at one or to the other, and see the Holy Spirit, and we ask of you to look upon your land one to the other, and see the Holy Spirit. And we ask of you to look upon the land and see the soil and the plants, and the minerals and the beauties—the animals, the reptilians, that which flies—all, all, all, every aspect that your beautiful eyes can see, and every aspect that your beautiful mind can wonder about, is the essence of Being.

You found as She spoke, a relaxed state in yourselves, did you not?

Marina: Yes, indeed.

Kevin: Yes.

Malachi: *You were vulnerable.*

Marina: Right.

Malachi: *In such state, you are impressed with Peacefulness, with the great Love. It is now moving through you in new conscious awareness. Every time you receive unto yourself the Holy Spirit, a new awareness recycles through your conscious[ness] and will be used by you. To be used, again, calls you into action, so you can express the potentiality of the Holy Spirit.*

You may allow yourselves to realize, [that] to have the Holy Spirit speaking with you, you have allowed it to surface stronger to your cognitive states. We shall say to you, you will let this surfacing continue to your cognitive states, that you will have what you term fresh ideas. You may call it inspirations. Fresh ideas. Fresh ideas will help you understand what will guide you through your healing modalities. Be vulnerable, then be active. Be receptive, then live what you allowed to surface. [Chuckling] *Now, beautiful ones, you have questions here?*

Kevin: One question I had was, will people who either hear what we just did, or listen to a recording of what we just heard with you and Holy Spirit—will they be able to have the same reaction, and the same ability to receive the Holy Spirit that we just had?

Malachi: *They will. The opportunity is available to them, is it not?*

Kevin and Marina: Yes.

Malachi: *Shall they be—what? Receptive? Were not of yourselves receptive?*

Kevin: Oh yes.

Malachi: *If they are not receptive, they receive unto themselves the Holy Spirit nonetheless. They may leave it locked in the unconscious, yet they are receiving the blessing.*

As you sit there amongst yourselves, what is continuing to move through your cellular essence? What do you feel?

Kevin: I feel like that vibration, a moving vibration. My brain feels different. I can't explain it totally, but it doesn't feel like it's wired the same now.

Marina: I feel that it's been re-wired. [All laugh]

Malachi: *You* ***are*** *re-wired. Do notice how this vibration will continue to carry through you. And whenever you gift of yourself a pausing moment, a recalling moment of the Holy Spirit, you'll feel these vibrations again.*

You are becoming aware of the Holy Spirit within you, that is you, that is Allness. And the more, again, [that] you have awareness, [then] the more you entrain your personal consciousness to the Holy Spirit consciousness.

And again, the more entrained, [then] the more Peaceful, harmonious energy you feel. You will not fall asleep. You will utilize this energy, utilize it in this field of the collective conscious of yourself, humanity, and yourself [as] an individual component living through this sphere, this beautiful sphere of manifestation.

All right, beautiful ones. Once again, we shall choose to leave the body, in the grace of allowing you to continue to feel the field of the Holy Spirit.

Marina: Thank you very much.

Kevin: Thank you, Malachi.

Chapter Twelve

Malachi, the Voice of Wisdom

You're the angels embodied. You are the Christ embodied. You are Source having a very great time, creating.

~ Malachi

Here I would like to explain more about Malachi and our relationship with him. He is an Ascended Master, which means that he has many times gone through this great course we call life on Earth, and graduated with the highest honors. He has continued in his service to the Holy Spirit, and has been with Jesus and Saint Germain since his ascension from Earth.

The Lives of the Ascended

All of the Ascended Masters once lived as ordinary people. But over the course of many Earth lives, they achieved a very high level of soul growth that led to a high level of enlightenment. Their ascension abilities enable them to travel to the Earth plane or to Heaven without their having to experience either physical birth or death.

These Masters have reached full awareness of their intrinsic union with the Divine. They are able to absorb and transmit very high levels of Light frequencies, and have been sending many such frequencies to the Earth to assist Her in Her ascension to a higher dimension.

These Masters of Higher Wisdom have lived Earth lives in many different places around the world, experiencing many different ethnicities and cultures. Though they are known by the names they carried in their most famous lifetimes, they are not defined by those cultures, or by the religions or philosophies they founded or influenced during those lives. These were merely vehicles for their teachings and their transmissions of energy and higher wisdom.

Malachi's Earth Lives

Several of Malachi's lifetimes have been spent with Jesus and Saint Germain. He was with them when Jesus walked upon this Earth as the Christ. At that time, Malachi was one of Jesus' very close followers, and traveled with Him around the world. The details of that time will be described in our upcoming biography *Jesus, the Prince of Peace.*

Jesus has told us that Marina and I were living Earth lives at the time of His life as Jesus, though he was known then by the Hebrew form of his name, Yeshua. (In English, this translates to Joshua. Yeshua translated into Greek is Iēsous, pronounced YAY-zoos, from which we get the name Jesus.)

Marina and I were followers of Yeshua, as was Malachi. We may have met Malachi during that lifetime.

Malachi also lived with Saint Germain and me in the 1500s, when we were all members of the Knights Templar, a guild that protected the wisdom and lineage of Jesus and the Holy Mother. At the end of that lifetime, Malachi reached Christ consciousness and ascended—he was taken up from this realm of matter into the higher spiritual realms, without having to physically die.

In another lifetime, he wrote the Book of Malachi in the Old Testament. In yet another life, lived during the twelfth century, he was Saint Malachy, the Archbishop of Armagh in Ireland. During that life he wrote "The Prophesy of the Popes," a document written in Latin that predicted the names of future Catholic popes with great accuracy, beginning in the mid-twelfth century and into the twentieth century.

I have also learned from Saint Germain that Malachi has now been raised to the level of Archangel. The Holy Spirit has bestowed this grand title upon him for his excellent service to humanity.

Learning from Malachi

Malachi has been speaking through the Oracle for more than thirty-five years. It is amazing that so few have brought this Divine Being's teachings into the public eye.

When a person is speaking to Malachi, they are speaking to God as well, because Malachi is in blended consciousness with the Holy Spirit, Jesus, Saint Germain, the Archangels and all of the members of the Great White Brotherhood of Light.

Each member maintains their individuated personality or energy signature, but at the same time, they are blended into the One. The One is God, and the totality of the Oneness is the Holy Spirit.

Malachi has brought this divine information to us since 2011. Every week, Malachi takes us a bit deeper into an understanding of the great mysteries of existence.

The following session is from April 2012. At this time, I was coming into the realization that we were speaking not only to Malachi the Archangel, but to many other beautiful Divine Beings.

From Session 47 on 4.9.12:

Kevin: Is Jesus part of you? Part of what you call the Group consciousness?

Malachi: *Indeed.*

Kevin: And Saint Germain?

Malachi: *Indeed, indeed.*

Kevin: And the one we call Mother Mary?

Malachi: *Indeed. And those with whom you would call the remarkable White Brotherhood. Do you understand?*

Kevin: Slightly.

Malachi: *Well, what is that [the Great White Brotherhood]? Well, we shall tell you.*

It is a group of grand souls that have been very familiar with the Earth, its structure, its building, its world upon world [that] it has experienced. Every soul has had the opportunity to live upon the Earth, and every soul has had the opportunity to bring light unto the Earth.

And every soul of the White Brotherhood holds the matrix of the Earth, and frequently we all can have a giggle when human beings believe they are going to destroy their Earth. You cannot. You can help it shape-shift, but you will not destroy it.

Kevin: Mother Theresa said that.

Malachi: *Indeed. So, you will do what? Blend with them all! For in there, that truly is what is called your heart, your soul desire, to be in the higher order of consciousness. To live in the beauty, your soul decided it would live on the Earth plane many times over. Until what? Do you know until what?*

Kevin: Until I ascend to the higher realm?

Malachi: *No, indeed, until you have the realization that it [the Earth] is a very beautiful and sacred place of soul evolution. That it is a very beautiful place, and that all of you that live in the individuated soul component are here to Love it, to Love your Earthly experiences, and to bring it all to harmony and to Light.*

When you have that knowing, you become enlightened. And in the enlightened reality, you can come and go at will. It is then a high choice, not a choice to balance out a karma, not a choice to keep balancing, in the seesaw of oppositions. Do you understand?

But the choice to stand at the regality of Earth and realize you are the knighted ones, the anointed ones, the high conscious ones. You're the Angels embodied, you are the Christ embodied. Do you understand?

You are Source having a very great time, creating. Does that help you?

Kevin: Oh yes.

My wife and I love Archangel Malachi, and look forward to every session, much like a college student looks forward to going home for the holidays to see their mother and father. He is a supreme intellect, a delightful vibration of Love, and a gentle and humorous teacher of the great mysteries.

Mother Mary in Earth History

The next two chapters offer an abundance of information that demonstrates some of what has been revealed here by Mother Mary and Malachi, including:

- How Mother Mary has been perceived by the Church over the centuries—Her historic titles, metaphors and descriptions

- How some of the historic titles given to Mary indicate that some of the Church's leaders may have known Her true identity as the Holy Spirit

- How from the early fourth century on, the established Church ensured that Mary's true identity as the Holy Spirit was hidden and deemed heretical

- How the truth of the Divine Feminine, as both Holy Spirit and ultimate Essence of all existence, was erased from the official Christian religion, after several centuries of common acceptance

- How great modern scholars such as Elaine Pagels have demonstrated how that the Divine Feminine came to be denounced by the established Church

It may take time to digest the fact that you have been reading the pure words of God the Holy Spirit, as well as the living words of Jesus the Christ and many other Divine Beings. The information in the following chapters is here to assist you in absorbing this groundbreaking Divine truth.

Chapter Thirteen

Mother Mary, Known by Many Names

I entered the field to help the human field remember the power of Love, the graciousness of community.

~ Mother Mary, the Holy Spirit

People around the world have long honored Mother Mary as a great Light, a Saving Grace, and a Divine Guide. Popes, saints and Christian writers have described Her in these terms for centuries.

The Holy Mother has been given many names in many different cultures. Nearly all of these names or metaphors lead to the revelation of Her role as Creator and Divine Mother.

In the Book of Mormon, for example, the prophet Nephi, who has a strong belief in Jesus, asks his angelic guide to tell him the meaning of the Tree of Life, which he and his father have seen in a vision. The answer he receives is found in the first book of Nephi, chapter 11: "An angel showed him a vision of the virgin Mary in Nazareth, and the mission and life of her son Jesus."

Brigham Young University Professor Daniel Peterson comments that Nephi knew that the Tree of Life represented the Canaanite goddess Asherah, the "mother of the gods" whose symbol is a tree trunk or a grove of trees. Nephi makes the connection between Asherah and Mother Mary. As he recounts his vision, Nephi calls Mary "the Mother of God."

Peterson comments that this is similar to the vision Saint Paul describes in II Corinthians 12:1-4, where Mary arrives in "great glory" in Her rightful place as Divine Mother, accompanied by angels singing Her praises.

The fourth century Gnostic text the Apocalypse of Paul describes Paul being shown a tree "in the midst of Paradise" called the Tree of Life. As he is looking at the tree, he sees "a virgin coming from afar and two hundred angels before her saying hymns." He asks, "'Sir, who is she who comes in so great glory?' And he was told: This is Mary the Virgin, the Mother of the Lord." [The Apocalypse of Paul, 46]

Mother Mary has also been called the Mediator between humankind and Jesus. This is true, but for a different reason than most people have assumed. We know now that our Mother God, the Holy Spirit, is the Presence that enables us to reach the Christ consciousness.

The Church has unintentionally given Mother Mary many titles that give Her the status of co-Creator, equal in Divinity to God the Father and Jesus. Other religions have called the Divine Mother the Divine Birther of creation.

By whatever name She is called, She is still God, the Holy Spirit, the Source from which all life flows, and which we are all a part of.

Though the early Christians understood Mother Mary's identity as Holy Spirit, that title has not been granted Her by the Church for many centuries. Since the third century CE, the grand realization that the Holy Mother is the Holy Spirit has been covered up and swept under the carpet of time. Yet we can see that there were Popes, teachers and scribes of religious thought who knew the truth of who She was.

The Popes' Titles for Mary

The popes of the sixteenth century gave Mother Mary numerous titles that indicated Her Divinity, in veiled ways. Pope Leo XIII called Her Our Lady of Light, a Safe Harbor of Travelers, and Mother of the Church.

In the Litany of the Blessed Virgin, Pope Sixtus V gave Mother Mary titles such as Queen Assumed into Heaven, Queen of Peace, and Queen of all Saints, Patriarchs, Angels, Prophets, Apostles and Martyrs.[1]

But how is She to be above all persons, including saints, prophets and Angels, and not be Divine?

Church leaders began calling Mary "Queen of Heaven" in the sixth century. In 1954, Pope Pius XII, known as the most Marian pope in Church history, made Queen of Heaven Her official title.[2]

As many popes have, Pius XII dubbed Mary Queen

because of Her earthly experience as Jesus' Mother. Because of the many early writings and teachings that he had access to in the Vatican, he may have privately known of Mary's Divine status, including the fact that it is even greater than that of Jesus. But he did not reveal this to the world.

Pius XII granted that Mary worked alongside Jesus, saying that She is "forever associated to Him, with a practically unlimited power, in the distribution of the graces which flow from the Redemption."[3] But he did not admit that She is redemption or rebirth itself.

Intercessory Power

In the old cathedrals of Europe, the Lady Chapel, dedicated to Mother Mary, is located behind the choir and the high altar, placing Mary in an intercessory position between God and humanity. [4]

Pius XII described Mary as being deserving of the Queenship "because she is Mother of God" a "New Eve with Jesus' redemptive work" with "intercessory power."[5] Royal status was officially granted Her because of Her Divine Motherhood.

We have been told through the centuries that Mary's Queenship is a "consequence of her being united with her Son, her being in heaven, in communion with God."[6] But we know now that She is more than Queen of Heaven. As Mother God, the Divine Feminine, She resides over all of creation, including the higher dimension of heaven.

The official Church has always given the Holy

Mother a subordinate role—higher than angels but lower than God the Father and Jesus. Christians are taught that the Holy Spirit is male, excluding all possibility that that Spirit could be Mother Mary.

Yet She is often exalted as having the role of Mediator or Intercessor, as well as Counselor and Comforter—a role that Church tradition has always attributed to the Holy Spirit, and which are attributed to no one else but the Holy Mother.

Divine Motherhood

Through the centuries, popes have granted Mother Mary the status of Divine Motherhood because She was the Mother of Jesus. That title was granted early on and established as the official history of the Church. The veiled (or accidental) message there, is that She is actually the Divine Mother of All.

In 1999, Pope Paul VI referred to Mary as Mother of the Church and the Queen of Peace, as well as Mother of Jesus and our Mother."[7] Again, this could be read as Divine Mother or Holy Mother, equal to God the Father, though no pope in history has ever fully admitted that Mary is also the Mother of Creation.

Perhaps that meaning was always there, left to be absorbed into our heart-minds as truth, though our head-minds often miss it entirely.

In 2012, Pope Benedict XVI described Mother Mary as watching over Her children, who look to Her for "maternal protection and heavenly assistance."[8] Over the centuries, many millions have been taught to pray to Mother Mary for help when they are lost, despairing, alone or seeking wisdom, in the same way that they have been taught to view the Holy Spirit as their Help and Guide.

We know by what has been revealed in this book, that this is correct, but in a much bigger way than what Benedict revealed. We are empowered in every aspect of our lives when we realize the I Am presence of the Holy Spirit.

For many centuries, humankind was told that God is a Presence separate from us, One we are not worthy to approach, except through Jesus. Mother Mary's Divine status empowers us to realize our own Divinity, our Oneness with one another, and our Oneness with All-That-Is.

Ascended Master

In 1950, Pope Pius XII declared the Assumption of Mary as a dogma. Once Mary had completed Her earthly life, "She was assumed body and soul into heavenly glory."[9] This was an official recognition of Mother Mary as an Ascended Master, though the Church would never have used that title.

The Church has never tried to explain how the Holy Mother came to have the status required to birth Jesus, the third member of the Holy Trinity. We are only taught that She was "overshadowed by the Holy Spirit" and that She was descended from the royal line of King David.

We know now that Mother Mary's decision to birth

Christ was based on Her desire to provide humankind an example of Christ consciousness:

> *From the realm of non-matter, the desire was birthed to bring to the realm of matter, a loving existence. To reveal to cultures a loving power, to bend a presence of consciousness, to impress, as your world says, to the collective field, to impress a consciousness of Love. In the essence of separation, the human field had been more of what you call war, harm, separation.*
>
> *I entered the field to help the human field remember the power of Love, the graciousness of community.*

There was no "overshadowing" of some other Divine Spirit before Jesus was conceived. Mary was fully conscious of Her Divine role, as Malachi describes, during Her pregnancy and even before it. She had constant knowledge and "acceptance of what the life growth was going to reveal."

Before Jesus' birth, She maintained "a matrix of thought energy and emotional energy that supported the intentions of the great change of humanity, through the agent of the Child called Jesus."

Intercessor and Companion

In a 1999 homily, Pope John Paul II called Mary "intercessor and companion" to Christ and the Church. He describes Her as advocate, evangelizer and intercessor for humankind—a Divine role.[10]

John Paul II notes this in his 1986 encyclical, in which he called Mary "this Spirit of truth whom Jesus calls the Paraclete." Paraclete is from the Greek word *parakletos,* meaning counselor, intercessor and advocate. [11]

John Paul II recalls that, "The era of the Church began with the descent of the Holy Spirit" and notes that all of the Apostles were gathered in the Upper Room in Jerusalem "together with Mary, the Lord's Mother."[12] He admits that Mary is integral to this vital moment.

He describes the work of the Holy Spirit as Intermediary and also notes that the "incarnation of the Son-Word" came about "by the power of the Holy Spirit." He calls Spirit the One "who gives life,"[13] referring in a veiled way to the Divine Giver of Life and Divine Birther—the Divine Mother, who created the incarnation of the Son-Word.

The Divine Feminine is not entirely missing from scripture or from Church mandates. Both have honored the Divine Feminine, but in a veiled way that few have decoded.

Wisdom and the Tree of Life

The scholar John A. Tvedtnes has noted that in the Eastern churches, Mary is sometimes identified with Hagia Sophia, who is "Holy Wisdom." As we've seen in an earlier chapter, Proverbs 3:18 calls Wisdom "a tree of life."

He sees a strong connection between Mary and the image of the Tree of Life in the early Christian Church. Many scholars have also found connections that indicate that the early Christians knew that the Wisdom of the Proverbs, the Tree of Life, and the Divine Mother Mary were all one.[14]

Proverbs 8:22-23 names Wisdom as being the Holy Spirit, just as Malachi has. As Creator, Mother Mary is described as having existed before anything else: "I, wisdom, was with the LORD when he began his work, long before he made anything else. I was created in the very beginning, even before the world began."

Mother of God

In 431 CE, the Council of Ephesus gave Mary the official title of *Theotokos*—Mother of God or God-Bearer.[15] This term was used by many early Church fathers to describe Mother Mary.

As Jesus is quoted often in the Gospels as stating, "I and the Father are one," Theotokos implies that even the Father came from the Divine Mother Mary.

Morning Star and Star of the Sea

Early Church fathers, scribes and visionaries often granted Mary the title of Morning Star, as Jesus is also called.

In a 2013 homily, Pope Francis asked, "Who is She that cometh forth as the morning rising, fair as the moon, bright as the sun?" He describes the Holy Mother as She is described throughout Church history—as Comforter and Counselor.[16]

She was first called Our Lady of Light during the

Middle Ages. Tradition holds that She Herself suggested the title to Saint Thomas of Canterbury.

Though third century Church father Origen did not allow women an active role in the Church, he gave Mary the title Domina or Lady, a feminine form of Lord. Other early Church fathers such as Saint Jerome and Saint Peter Chrysologus did the same.[17]

The title "Sweet Star of the Sea" has been used to describe the Divine Mother for centuries in shrines, hymns and writings throughout Europe. Saint Ephraim called Mary "the safe harbor of all sailing on the sea of the world." Saint Bonaventure spoke to those who had fallen from the ship of Divine grace, telling them not to despair, but to cast their eyes "on this beautiful star for it will guide you into the port of salvation." [18]

In the early 1600s, the mystic Saint Mary Magdalen of Pazzi had a vision in which she saw a vessel that held "all the clients of Mary, and Mary Herself steering the ship into port."[19] Mary is constantly described in the role of the Holy Spirit, interceding on behalf of humanity.

Saint Gertrude the Great prayed, asking Jesus that in her last hour, He would send to her "Thy tender Mother Mary, that soft-shining Star of the Sea, that She may stand by me as my sure defense."[20]

In the twelfth century, a famous shrine was built in Marseilles, France, after fishermen there nearly drowned when their boat was caught in a storm. The men appealed to Mother Mary for help by singing the hymn "Ave Maris Stella"—"Hail, Star of the Sea." They were saved from the storm, and later described seeing Mary at the wheel, guiding their boat to safety.

A chapel was built on the coast nearby, and a statue erected called Our Lady of Mariners. Mother Mary is honored there as Protectress of Marseilles with the title "the Star above the storms."[21]

These sailors, like so many through the ages, intuitively recognized Mary as the Divine Mother. As the Holy Mother has explained to us, we are never alone. She is always with us.

The Fountain of Living Water

Mother Mary has long been called a Fountain or Well of Living Water. Many have referred to Mary's Divinity by describing Her as the Living Waters.

The third century bishop Saint Gregory described Mary as "the ever-flowing fountain" in which "the water of life sprang and produced the Lord's incarnate manifestation . . . the life-bearing plant."[22]

Perhaps without meaning to, he was equating Mary with the Holy Spirit, the ever-flowing Fountain of Life and Birther of creation.

Queen of All Things

An encyclical by Pius XII quotes Saint Anselm, who in the eleventh century wrote that as God "is Father and Lord of all," Mary is Mother and Queen of all, "the Queen of all things, because she restores each to its original dignity through the grace which she merited."[23]

"Queen of all things" implies Creator of all things. Mother Mary as Holy Spirit has indeed birthed us, and restores us to our original dignity by working within the Divine grid of Light and energy that holds the codes of perfection for every life and object.

She heals our souls by releasing all lower and negative energies from us. She heals our physical bodies by accessing the Divine DNA and RNA that exists in all living beings, as Jesus did when he enacted his miraculous healings.

The Woman Clothed with the Sun

Through the centuries, the Church has also identified Mary as the woman described as "clothed with the sun" in the Book of Revelation:

> A great and wondrous sign appeared in heaven: a woman clothed with the sun, with the moon under her feet and a crown of twelve stars on her head. She was pregnant and cried out in pain as she was about to give birth. [Revelation 12:1-3 NIV]

This is an image of Mother Mary, the Divine Feminine, birthing our New World.

The Crown of Twelve Stars

The Holy Mother is often pictured in religious art as the Madonna of the Star, wearing a crown of twelve stars. The stars are shown as embroidered on Her veil or on the right shoulder of Her blue mantle. She is depicted as the Morning Star, Star of the Sea, Star of Jacob and the Fixed Star.

The hymn for the Feast of the Most Holy Rosary states, "Twelve stars now crown the brow of the glorious Mother; near the throne of her Son she reigns over all created things."[24]

When Mother Mary appeared to the children at Pontmain, France in 1871, they also described Her as having been surrounded by stars.[25]

The crown of twelve stars is a reference to the sign of Virgo, the Latin term for virgin. In the astrological tradition, Mother Mary is symbolic of the Virgo constellation. In this new age we've entered, the Divine Feminine is again coming forward to be as activated as the Divine Masculine, in the cosmos and in human consciousness.

A clear sign of this occurred with the Venus Transit, on June 5, 2012. During this six-hour event, the planet Venus traveled across the face of the sun, something that only happens once about every 113 years or so. Venus is associated with the astrological sign of Virgo, which is personified by Mother Mary.[26]

The energies activated by that astrological and astronomical event were extremely important. They opened an aspect of the heart chakra that allows us to connect with our souls and our own Divinity in a new and empowering way.

During this event, the Sun's light, imbued with the golden Light of the Christ consciousness, merged with the Light energy of Venus, the Divine Feminine.

Venus is also known by the names Queen of Heaven, Isis, Aphrodite, and Mother Mary. This union of the Divine Masculine Light of the Sun with the Divine

Feminine Light of Venus was an outer manifestation of the Divine Father and Divine Mother joining energies, with Earth serving as Christ or creation, the third point in the triangle or trinity. [27]

The Gift of the Divine Mother

The Light coming to the Earth during that six-hour window activated the sacred geometries embedded in our cellular DNA, taking both our consciousness and our physical bodies to a higher vibrational level. This Light activated within us is the energies of the Divine harmony, Love and Light being radiated by Venus and the sun.

The activation came to Earth via the Rose Ray, a particularly high form of Light. The Rose Ray contains the sacred geometry required to reactivate the strands of our DNA that were deactivated thousands of years ago by the dark forces. This deactivation made ascension to the higher spiritual levels nearly impossible for the majority of human beings, until now. [28]

This transmission of Light and healing is a gift from Mother Mary the Holy Spirit, so that we can align with the Divine codes of creation. These codes contain the Shekinah (Divine Mother/Holy Spirit) and Mother Mary code of the Sacred Heart.

The transmissions bring concentrated healing on a cellular level, and enable us to absorb the higher frequencies of Light in a way that won't send our physical bodies into shock.[29]

This Light is also a form of protection given us by the Divine Mother, during the years from 2012 to 2014, in which Earth is being cleansed of the lower vibrations and entities that have disabled human spiritual potential for thousands of years.

This very empowering Light and energy transmission also carries the Divine power of the Blue Ray Light transmissions. These enable regeneration on a cellular level, bringing humankind more into alignment with our higher path.[30]

Except for a few saints and mystics, no era of Church or human history could have envisioned before now the power of this special aid, comfort and protection. It is a great ascension gift, given to us by our Divine Mother, the Holy Spirit.

Chapter Fourteen

Intentional Misinformation: Hiding Mother Mary's Divine Identity

Come, hidden Mother;
Come, thou that art manifest in thy deeds.
~ Acts of Thomas 5:50

In their book *Mary Magdalene and the Divine Feminine: Jesus' Lost Teachings on Woman,* Annice Booth and Elizabeth Clare Prophet look at the meaning of another title the Church gave Mother Mary in the 1960s, after the first moon landing: Mother of the Universe.

Most etymologists agree that the word "matter" (created substance) is derived from the Latin word *mater*, which is "mother." That is not an accident. The Divine Mother is Creator of all matter, the Divine Birther of All-That-Is.[1]

Many indigenous peoples around the world refer to the Divine as Mother Earth and Father Sky. They know that both masculine and feminine energies are required for creation. This was also understood by the early Christians.

It was known to Jesus and His followers that Mother Mary was the Divine Mother, the Holy Spirit. So then how were these teachings lost to the world?

Hidden History

Elaine Pagels is a professor of religion at Princeton University and an expert on Gnostic writings. She describes how the early founders of the established Church removed all references to the Divine Feminine from Church teachings, and removed women from any involvement in Church order and ritual.

This was a complete turnaround from how the Christian movement had begun. Though it violated Hebrew tradition, Jesus had spoken openly with women on the streets. He treated them as equals in His teaching, in the temple, and by including women in His group. But from the year 200 CE onward, Pagels tells us, there is no evidence that women were in "prophetic, priestly, and episcopal roles among orthodox churches."[2]

The early Christians did follow Jesus' example, and allowed women leadership and teaching roles in the very early Church. But while women were at first allowed a practical role, the Feminine was soon denied a Divine role.

Pagels writes that the orthodox churchmen decided that "the teachings on the Divine Mother and the feminine principle were not the true teachings of Jesus Christ." They were therefore not included in the canon of scripture that became the New Testament in the early third century.

All teachings and scripture that did not support a completely patriarchal tradition were eliminated from the canon. By the year 200 CE, Pagels notes, "virtually all the feminine imagery for God had disappeared from orthodox Christian tradition."[3]

Author Rosemary Radford Ruether describes the idea of a feminine Holy Spirit as "too much a female deity for patriarchal Christian orthodoxy."[4]

The Gnostic Gospels and the Divine Feminine

The Gnostics were an early Christian sect. They believed that the way to grace was to have insight and understanding (gnosis) of God and of the soul, or of the higher self as God, as well as knowledge of the universe itself.[5]

The Gnostics were many different groups under one banner, and especially thrived during the second century. Their teachings were based on the idea that we already have within us all we need to know God. The Gnostics did not believe the vengeful, angry God of the Old Testament was the true God, and named him "the Demiurge." They saw no need for a belief in separation between humans and the Divine.

The Gnostic Gospel of Thomas quotes Jesus as saying that there is no need for a human intermediary or an Earthly hierarchy—we can come to know God on our own. They also placed Mother Mary as Divine Mother at the heart of their teachings.

Then the Roman Emperor Constantine decreed

Christianity to be the official religion of Rome in 313 CE. During that era, the theologian Tertullian wrote that women were "the devil's gateway." He blamed humankind's separation from God on women, claiming, "you are the unsealer of that [forbidden] tree: you are the first deserter of the divine law: you are she who persuaded him whom the devil was not valiant enough to attack." He goes on to credit women with having "destroyed so easily God's image, man," and blames them for the crucifixion of Jesus.[6]

The Church upheld Tertullian's teachings, and the concept of the Divine Feminine was forbidden in mainstream Christian teaching. Though Gnostic teachings continued, they were considered heretical.

The Church became part of the Roman city-state, creating an official canon and creeds that were enforced with political and military force. In this time, as Malachi has described, "religious and governmental heads were one and the same." The Church began to actively suppress and try to destroy Gnostic writings and teachings.

The Truth Reappearing

For centuries, the early writings of the Gnostic Christians were destroyed by Church authorities or hidden in the Vatican libraries. But by the mid-twentieth century, evidence of early Christian belief in Mother Mary as Mother God began to re-emerge.

In 1945, ancient manuscripts were discovered near Nag Hammadi, Egypt. The thirteen papyrus volumes revealed fifty-two early Gnostic Christian writings, mostly written during the third and fourth century.

They offer a very different view of the life and teachings of Jesus compared to what the Church has offered humankind since the third century. Because they are Gnostic writings, the Nag Hammadi texts also speak of a God who is Divine Mother as well as Divine Father.

In her book *The Gnostic Gospels*, Elaine Pagels writes that the Gnostic writings depict God as Mother in three distinct ways: as part of an original couple; as the Holy Spirit or Third Person of the Trinity; and as Wisdom.

Due to the suppression of the truth of Mother Mary's identity, the idea that God could be both Father and Mother is still unacceptable to millions. Yet the present canon of scripture contains many names and images that confirm the truth of the Divine Feminine.

This is despite the fact that the early Church fathers removed or changed many of these references. The texts were also intentionally made more masculine during the centuries before the printing press, when monks and scribes interpreted, translated and copied out the scriptures by hand.

The Essenes and the Gnostics

The Essenes, the ancient Hebrew sect that Jesus was born into, had much in common with the early Gnostic Christians. The Essenes lived a life of extreme simplicity, living in community as one family and sharing all possessions.

They took nothing with them when they traveled, as they would stay with other Essenes who would provide all they needed. All food, clothing and shelter were provided within their community, so that Hebrew law would be followed on all levels of daily living.

They believed in mercy, honesty and purity of mind and heart. They were peacemakers who shunned all concept of war or weapons, and who banned slavery among themselves. Brotherly love and service to others were central to how they lived their everyday lives.[7]

The Essenes were also healers of both body and soul. They strove to heal and to cast out evil spirits miraculously, to foresee events and to prophesy.

Everyone in the Essene community worked and lived at an equal social and spiritual level, without any hierarchy. Each day, they would draw lots to determine who would offer sacraments, read the sacred texts, and prophesy or teach for that day.[8]

This was the community that Jesus (called Yeshua) was raised in. Like the Essenes, He also stressed equality among people, performed miraculous healings and prophesied. He raised the law of Divine Love above any Earthly hierarchy, and stressed the inherent equality among all people, including between men and women.

Church Orthodoxy and the Divine Feminine

In September 2012, the world media reported on the discovery of a fragment of a Coptic papyrus that contains the quote: "Jesus said to them, 'My wife . . . she will be able to be my disciple.'" Elaine Pagels commented on this discovery in an interview on National Public Radio.

Professor Pagels noted that there are more than fifty texts that came from the early Christian movement in the first few centuries. Many of these were "secret gospels" that have only been published within the last few decades.

She went on to say that during the first 400 years of Christianity, people read many different Christian writings, including the Gnostic texts (before the official New Testament canon was chosen by the Council of Laodicea around 363 CE). This included the Gnostic Gospel of Thomas, in which Jesus speaks of "my mother, the Holy Spirit." This gospel was widely read until it was left out of the official canon.[9]

The great diversity of information available in those days about Jesus and His teachings was considered a dangerous threat by the Church, which permitted only one official set of beliefs. This process began with Constantine and his bishops. These churchmen created a canon of what they said were authorized teachings. The rest were called heretical.[10]

The Gnostic Gospels of Mary, Philip, Judas and Thomas, which all speak of both a Mother God and a Father God, were all excluded from the canon.

Church orthodoxy sought to control how people related to God, to one another and to outer authority. The Gnostic teachings taught independence from any hierarchy.

They were viewed by rulers such as Irenaeus and the theologian Tertullian as a danger to the newly established order.

Prominent Gnostic theologians who challenged the Church's canon, such as Marcion, were labeled as heretics.[11]

Yin-Yang as Father-Mother God

The Gnostics taught that human beings were created in the image of the Divine. Since the Divine had created both sexes, they reasoned that God must also be both male and female. The Gnostic writings describe the Divine as a masculine/feminine blend of opposites, similar to the Eastern view of yin and yang.

One of the Divine Mother's Earthly incarnations was as the Chinese Goddess of Mercy and Compassion, Quan Yin (or Kwan Yin), who is honored in different forms throughout Asia.

The Asian yin-yang symbol, a circle containing equal amounts of light and dark, can be viewed as a symbol of spirit and matter, or male and female. It represents the balance between the Divine Feminine and the Divine Masculine in Eastern thought and beliefs. There is no equivalent for this in Western Christian tradition, except in Gnosticism.

Hinduism and the Divine Feminine

Author and Hinduism expert David Frawley sees the Gnostic concept of Father-Mother God as similar to the Hindu teaching of a Divine Male and Divine Female. This is represented by a Hindu God and His shakti (wife or consort), who is the creative force in the universe. [12]

There is a profound belief in the Divine Mother in the cultures of the Far East. A thousand-year-old stone sculpture on Elephanta Island in India portrays the figure of the Hindu God Shiva as male on one side and female on the other. It is known as Ardhanarishvara, "the Lord who is both male and female."[13]

The Vedas are the earliest scriptures of Hinduism, written between 1500 and 1000 BCE. The oldest Hindu text, the Rig Veda, refers to the Divine Father and Divine Mother as Heaven and Earth—Mother Earth and Father Sky—just as many Native American cultures have.

The Gnostic writings recorded that Jesus studied the teachings of the Eastern sages and Buddhas. They describe how he traveled to sacred places in the Far East, such as Tibet. One of the ideas He brought back, and no doubt shared with His disciples, was the belief in the Divine Mother, which would also have been taught to Him by the Holy Mother.[14]

Mother Mary has told us that these "lost years" of Jesus' life, when He was between the ages of thirteen and thirty, were never actually lost. The information was simply buried long ago, with the Gnostic gospels.

The Vedic Indian concept of Vac also relates strongly to Mother Mary. Vac is many things—the sounds of nature and animals, of prayer and human speech, and of holy speech, personified. She is also a Goddess.

Booth and Prophet comment that if a Hindu were to hear Jesus described as the incarnate Word, they would understand it as Jesus being the incarnation of the Divine

Mother. They point out that Jesus held a "tremendous flame of the Divine Mother of love" and had "tremendous peace and caring for life."[15] Both the New Testament and Gnostic gospels make clear that Jesus' feminine aspect is perfectly balanced with His masculine aspect.

The Holy Spirit as She

Both orthodox and Gnostic writers who wrote in the ancient Syriac language used Divine Mother images to describe the Holy Spirit. In Syriac, Hebrew and Aramaic (which Jesus spoke), the word for spirit (*ruach*) is feminine. Like the Gnostics, the Semitic branch of early Christianity taught the femininity of the Spirit and Her Earthly role as Jesus' mother.[16]

This can also be seen in the writings of fourth-century theologians and in the early Syriac Christian writings. The Gnostic Acts of Thomas, from the early third century, also speak of a Divine Feminine. The "Holy Dove" in this writing is clearly the Holy Spirit:

> Holy Dove that bearest the twin young;
> Come, hidden Mother;
> Come, thou that art manifest in thy deeds
>
> Come and partake with us in this Eucharist
> Which we celebrate in thy name, and in
> the love-feast in which we are gathered
> together at thy call. [Acts of Thomas 5:50][17]

The apocryphal Gospel of the Hebrews also describes the Divine Feminine, in a fragment quoted by Origen and the very orthodox Saint Jerome: "Even so did my mother, the Holy Spirit, take me by one of my hairs and carry me away to the great mountain Tabor."[18]

The Gnostic Gospel of Philip also describes the Holy Spirit as Divine Mother, saying, "Her children are many."[19]

The Ancient Hebrews and the Divine Feminine

The ancient Hebrew writings of the Talmud speak of the Shekhinah, the cloud that descended into the tabernacle created by Moses as he led the Israelites through the desert. It is described as a God presence, a "cloud of glory that rested on the mercy seat in the Holy of holies."[20]

In the mystical teachings of the Jewish Kabbalah, the Shekhinah has a feminine aspect. The I Am presence is both Father and Mother God. One is Creator, and the other is the activating principle of that creation.[21]

The Zohar, the main text on Kabbalism, identifies the Shekhinah with the entire community of Israel, in a way that makes Her the Mother of everyone in Israel.[22] She is both the Divine Mother of the Israelites and Holy Spirit.

Islam and the Divine Feminine

In *Sophia: Goddess of Wisdom*, Caitlín Matthews describes how Sophia or Wisdom represents the Divine Feminine in Islam. She also notes that, "Both Mary and Fatima are reverenced within esoteric Islam, for they are both mothers of the Logos, the Word."[23]

Matthews quotes Ibn Arabi, the twelfth-century

Sufi mystic and philosopher. Arabi called universal nature *Tavi'at al-kull*, "the feminine or maternal side of the creative act." This maternal aspect is the "merciful 'breathing-out' of God." Sophia is "the Divine Sigh of Compassion in Sirach, the book of Wisdom."

Dervish Laurence Galian points out that just as God breathed upon the waters in Genesis during the act of creation, this "breathing out" manifests Sophia into the world, "yet Sophia is also the dwelling place of God." As the Divine Feminine who is the Creator, nothing can exist before Her.[24]

The Islamic thirteenth-century Sufi poet Rumi put it beautifully: "Woman is the radiance of God; she is not your beloved. She is the Creator—you could say that she is not created."[25]

Galian points out that the two most holy names in Islam are "Allah: al-Rahman and al-Rahim, which state that the Source of Life is the Divine Feminine."[26]

Missing the Divine Feminine

Among the religions of the world, Judaism and Christianity stand out as unusual. They offer no Divine Mother to balance the presence of the Divine Father.

In his sermon "The Divine Mother," Unitarian Universalist minister Rev. Rick Hoyt comments that the structure of Judeo-Christian tradition leaves us "motherless."

It is a culture that has spent the last 3,000 years picturing God almost exclusively as a Divine Father. This has left Western thinking to value only the purely rational, logical and aggressive, while intuition, compassion, mystery and the soul are downplayed and devalued.

We have separated reason from emotion, valuing reason far more highly than emotion. We have also separated "humanity from nature, and value human wants above nature's needs."[27]

He calls this "spiritually tragic." Though patriarchal religion was supposed to restore us to the paradise our Creator intended, "this is still quite different from the story our Divine Mother would have told us."

This is exactly what Malachi has revealed to us about the process of separation. "The more humanity continued to feel their dynamics of only humanness, their third-dimensional reality, the less they could comprehend the grander aspect of the Divine Feminine and the Divine Masculine."

Hoyt believes that we know intuitively that we have a Divine Mother, and that we still live in Her paradise. "She is the Earth beneath us and the Holy Feminine qualities within us." We don't need religion to give us a Divine Mother, "because religion hasn't the power to take her away. We can invoke Her for ourselves, if we need to."

He encourages us to "Seek Her within, as She silently but expectantly waits for you. . . the Mother you seek has always been close and leads inward to your own soul."[28]

Mother Mary Herself has assured us that no matter what we may have been taught, we have not been abandoned:

Source is always with you. You are never alone. You are always loved deeply and forever, no matter what. Learn how to love yourself. I tell you, that you are so worthy of the Great Love from the Divine. In reality, you are all just Pure Light and Love. Nothing else.

Humankind has now finished the last Earth cycle in which the masculine was allowed to dominate the feminine. As of December 21, 2012, we have entered a new age, in which the Divine Feminine will be weighed as equal in importance to the Divine Masculine. The veil of deception and hidden truths can no longer be sustained. Mother Mary is taking her natural place in our hearts as Mother God, the Holy Spirit.

Our Divine Mother has said that even though we choose separation, we have always carried the impulse to know the One God, the Source, the Holy Spirit. Over the centuries, we have given thousands of names to the Oneness of All.

As our Blessed Mother tells us:

I did not birth only one Child, to perform in the realm of matter what is seen as miracle, I have birthed all to be the miraculous reality of Oneness. Allow yourselves to be the miraculous Holy Spirit. The more you feel your Oneness, the more there is no worry. Peace prevails in your mind, in your endeavors.

Chapter Fifteen

A Conclusion Without an End

You are the living Holy Spirit.

~ Malachi

As I was finishing this book, I felt a strong urge to ask one of the Divine Beings for a statement that would serve as the conclusion of this holy book. I asked Malachi if anyone would like to come forward to give a statement.

Malachi immediately went quiet. The Oracle's posture and facial expression began to change. Marina turned to look at me with an excited smile, and I nodded. It was the Divine Mother Mary, coming through the Oracle.

There was a pause about a minute long, during which time I felt like a child getting ready to open his first gift on Christmas morning.

Then She spoke.

> *My child, there is no conclusion, for there's no end. There is only Grace. Your final statement: Be filled with Grace.*

Reading this later on, I felt Grace filling my being. I said, "I Am that I Am. I Am Grace."

Anu, Isis and Quan Yin

More information has since come to us from Malachi. He has told us that the Holy Spirit not only incarnated as Mother Mary and Quan Yin (or Kwan Yin). She also incarnated as Anu and Isis.

In each lifetime, Holy Spirit sought to bring balance, guidance and healing to places and times that were being ravaged by wars or misguided aggression. We will be releasing a book about the life and teachings of Quan Yin, called *The Goddess of Compassion and Mercy, Quan Yin.*

Anu was an ancient Celtic Goddess who was known as the Mother God, the ancestor of all Gods. It seems that the people of Her time knew She was the Holy Spirit.

Isis was the wife of Osiris and Mother of Horus, who was worshipped in his time as Jesus is now. It is said that Horus was born of a Virgin Mother. There are many similarities between Horus and Jesus, as there are between Mary and Isis. Now we know why: Mary and Isis were both direct incarnations of the Holy Spirit.

During the session in which Mother Mary told us that Holy Spirit incarnated more than just once, She instructed us to tell humanity that Holy Spirit is very much part of the human world.

Humans are not alone. They have never been, and never will be left alone. The Divine Mother is available to all of us at every moment in countless ways.

We all carry the capacity of Her abilities, Her Love, Her compassion, Her grace and Her magic. We have the power of creation at our fingertips. We can and will create a Divinely beautiful world of Peace and Love.

We will have Heaven on Earth.

From Session L86 on 8.28.13:

Malachi: *All right, beautiful beings. Breathe in deeply, to feel your own personalities. And in the feeling of your personality, feel your essence as Holy Spirit.*

Remind yourselves [that] you have been under quite a lesson, a continual lesson: Holy Spirit in matter. You have felt the beautiful blessings of Quan Yin. With Quan Yin, you have been able to identify [that She] was a human being who existed on the Earth, [and] was Mother Mary, a human being that existed on the Earth.

And yet your revelation [is] that that existence is nothing less than Oneness, Holy Spirit, and that lesson constantly returns unto you. You are the living Holy Spirit.

The vibrations that the Holy Spirit leaves upon the Earth plane, in the individual components, is a vibration that every human being, every essence—that includes your beautiful plants, animals and minerals of your Earth plane, the air that you breathe, the rains that you feel—all elements, [are] nothing but the Holy Spirit, in personification.

There is always a gift, a gift to help any quality of the Holy Spirit that has deepened its sleep, that has awakened even if [only] partially, or awakened fully.

In your world, you have a phrase: It is a journey. And it is a beautiful journey.

A Glossary of Light

Words of Light Used by the Angels

If I have said the earthly things to you, and ye believe not, how, if I say the heavenly things to you, will ye believe?

~ John 3:12
[Darby Translation]

Our human languages are not adequate to describe multi-dimensional existence, the higher realms, super-human abilities, and other concepts that transcend time and space. This makes it harder to comprehend channeled messages that attempt to explain the reality of the Divine realm.

This glossary is a resource for those seeking greater understanding of that realm. Take the time to absorb these meanings and the energy within them. They can help you in your journey of merging with the consciousness of the higher realms.

14,000 years ago: The point at which the human collective consciousness went through a process of separation; the end of the Golden Age

2,000 CE [Common Era]: The time of Jesus' birth as a human being

2,600 years ago - 600 BCE [Before the Common Era]: The planting of the New Garden; the seeding of the families of Mary and Joseph, and the beginning of the Divine Plan to bring forth a Christed One as an example for humankind as it enters the New Age

666 Gateway: The two-thirds of the human collective consciousness needed to manifest human awakening to the higher consciousness of Light, Peace, Unconditional Love, Compassion, Sharing and total awareness that All is One; the beginning of the Christed consciousness on Earth

70 CE: The year that Jerusalem was destroyed by fire

Age: A period of time spanning approximately 2,160 years

Agents of light: Spiritual trackers; those who represent the words and intentions of the Divine Beings

Agents: Mediators or representatives of higher consciousness, relaying higher frequencies of Light and energy to humanity

Akashic Records: A compendium of knowledge and information in the astral plane (the fifth dimension or Heaven), in which all things that have ever been thought, written, said, experienced or felt are recorded; accessible via the meditative state

Angelic Beings: Beings of higher Light and energy who radiate a higher Love to our Earth and throughout the universe; messengers and workers who carry out the Holy Spirit's work, answering prayers and aiding human beings who request their help

Antichrist: Fears, doubts and worries; not a person or being; whatever prevents one from knowing and merging with Source energy

Ascension: Graduating from the university that is life on Earth; raising one's awareness beyond the veils of consciousness that delineate the dimensions; merging one's consciousness with that of the higher realms

Ascension Vibration: Rays of Light and waves of energy sent from the higher realms to assist with humankind's rise to the fourth and fifth dimensions; blending with this higher energy enables higher states of consciousness, and a higher spiritual and emotional vibration

Asleep: Spiritually unawakened; existing in the illusion of separateness; asleep to the presence of the Holy Spirit or Source energy

Atlantis: A lost continent in the Atlantic Ocean, which thrived for centuries during the Golden Age, until its demise

Attempt: The action of trying to walk the path of spiritual growth and expansion; a recognizable action

Attosecond: One quintillionth of a second

Awaken: No longer in the illusion of separation; remembering through higher consciousness the Oneness of All; according to Saint Germain, tapping into the great collections of thought as well as physical processes that aid humankind's evolution, turning it toward a consciousness of Spirit

Being: The individual quality of one's existence; both inner consciousness and outer living

Blended consciousness: A merging of consciousness with those of another being, such as merging with that of the Masters, Archangels, Angels, the Oneness of All, or with any object or life form

Bliss: A high state of peaceful, joyful awareness; awareness of the harmony of Oneness; greater consciousness; total union

Bridges: Connections between the worlds and between human consciousness and Divine consciousness; crossing points between the Earthly consciousness and our sacred souls; remembering our I Am presence

Celibacy: Abstinence from sexual relations; according to Malachi, this is a path that does not lead to enlightenment or Oneness, but only to further separation

Cellular memory: The physical and spiritual unconscious

Cellular vibrations: Frequencies that affect us on a cellular level; necessary to shape-shift and change both body and brain; higher energy frequencies that help one become more aligned with Divinity

Center point: A focus on being the Divine embodied, reached by recalling true Source consciousness; an awareness of being/experiencing Peace and Unconditional Love

Children of the Divine: All of humanity; all extensions of the Divine Mother and Father living in this world

Christ: A title, not a name; from the Greek *Christos*, meaning messiah or anointed one; a pure state of consciousness

Christed awareness: A miraculous consciousness; the full awareness that one is Spirit in matter; not only carrying an intellectual awareness but fully embodying and living the Christ consciousness of the higher mind

Christed beingness: The vibration of Oneness and truth; our Christed intent to be, found when one is in center point

Christed consciousness: Living in the higher awareness of Oneness and Unconditional Love, which creates a ripple effect that is felt by the entire collective field of humanity

Christed self: Higher consciousness and higher awareness; living with faith, without worry, fear or doubt

Classroom: Earth, where human beings come to experience life's lessons for soul growth and expansion

Collective Soul: The consciousness of humanity, the field of awareness of all humans

Consciousness: Inner awareness; that within us which never dies; our conscious and subconscious self that is constantly seeking unity with Divine consciousness

Cycles: The universe's sequences, played out in time, in which the greater influences of feminine or masculine move in alternating patterns

Discernment: Using one's own heart and higher intuition to know what is true or not

Discombobulated: Feeling distress in the chakras and body; an unconscious response; to be out of center point; can occur when one receives an abundance of Divine Light

Divine energy: Perfect purity of the highest vibration that enables all life and positively charges the fields within us and around us

Divine Feminine: The feminine aspect of Source Energy; the highest compassion; a nurturing consciousness; the wisdom that is always birthing and nurturing the new and higher reality

Divine Love: True Source; unconditional acceptance; Sacred Fire; Source Consciousness; Divine harmony, consciousness and heart

Divine manifestation: Bringing the consciousness of the higher realms into the realm of matter; operating with Divinity to create and birth new matter or circumstances

Divine Masculine: The active component of the Holy Spirit; the attributes of Divine action, creation and doing

Divine Oneness: The I Am presence; the unifying principle of the One that runs through all of creation; the All-That-Is

Doorways: Portals or openings through which beings, forms of consciousness, and awareness can pass

Earth: A sacred place of the learning that is part of the experience of the evolution of the soul

Earth's ascension: The movement of the planet into higher levels of consciousness, toward the consciousness of Oneness; Earth's ascension into the fourth dimension began in 2012, formulated by Light rays and higher energies

Ego (higher): An aspect of the Higher Self, which has constant connection to and awareness of the Holy Spirit, carrying no consciousness of separateness

Ego (lower): The lower mind of Earthly consciousness, which must be risen out of in order to attain enlightenment; a state in which human beings are constantly vulnerable to manipulation and control by lower energies.

Energetic sensitivity: Having an awareness of energies coming into our physical and auric bodies.

Energy healing: Directing higher frequencies of Light and energy into a person's physical or auric body to free them of pain, injury or illness; also, releasing negative energies or blocks in energy in the physical or auric body

Energy signature: The unique code or pattern contained in every created form or being; the unique vibration of every component of Source.

Enlightenment: Conscious and profound awareness that all is Light and Spirit, whether it exists in the form of energy or matter; an individual soul living in harmony and Light, living according to higher consciousness; the understanding that all of humanity are Angels embodied, Christ embodied, a component of Source; a consciousness of the regality of Earth and Heaven

Eon: A full rotation of precession of the equinoxes, totaling 25,920 years; the most recent of these time periods ended in December 2012

Essenes: An ancient Hebrew sect; an ascetic community of holy men and women who carried ancient wisdom and the seeds of Christ; considered to be the writers of the Dead Sea Scrolls; the community that Mary, Joseph and Jesus were a part of

Evolution of Oneness: The process by which humanity comes to realize the truth of the Oneness of all

Evolutionary separation: The process by which humanity refused to see that all contain the spark of the Divine; the movement away from consciousness of union

Expanded union: The expansion of the consciousness of unity; allowing oneself to be open and receptive to the Divine on all levels

Family of Light: Every living being, for all are part of Source

Fearing God: A consciousness of separation from God; the belief that God is angry and inaccessible to human beings; in another sense, fearing oneself, since all are part of God

Feminine paradigm: The structure of thought that supports the Divine traits of nurturing, Love, compassion and birth; the experience of humanity of internal Peace, Unconditional Love and gentleness

Fifth dimension: The New World of higher consciousness; increasingly accessed by Earth now that the veils of separation are being removed; alignment with Divine Love; consciousness of and unity with the Holy Spirit in all things

Fourth dimension: The state of increased blending and increased awareness of the higher dimensions, Oneness with creation and one another; equates to the fourth strand of human DNA

Free choice: Free will; the individual path of each soul and its chosen experiences; respected by those in the higher realms

Free will zone: The world of matter; the place of choice for all individuals, to choose or reject the consciousness of Oneness, to choose or reject soul growth and expansion

Galactic brothers and sisters: Our ethereal friends from other dimensions and places in the multiverse, who serve higher levels of consciousness

Giving of Source: The act of God giving to God, as we are all God

Godhead: All that emerges from the Holy Spirit; the individual components of Holy Spirit; also, the acting consciousness of any person, object, spirit or Divine Source

Golden Age: The era in which humans were actively conscious of Oneness.

Golden Path: The path of consciousness, for those who are walking the path to greater awareness

Golden Work: The work of service, for Holy Spirit; the work of soul growth and expansion

Grand Trinity: The Holy Spirit (the Divine Mother), the Divine Father, and Jesus, in blended Oneness; the grid that defines the integrity of living in this holographic universe

Grand World: The ultimate reality; heaven; the world beyond the dimensions of the holographic universe, where the Divine beings reside; accessed by human beings through attainment of higher consciousness

Great Library: The Great Hall of Wisdom; accessible when one is in a meditative state, outside the constraints of the lower ego; a place of great learning, knowledge and wisdom; the place of the Book of Life and the Akashic Records

Great Light: Divine Energy and higher awareness; the highest Light

Great transition: The movement of one's awareness to the Light and higher intentions, higher consciousness

Great White Brotherhood of Light: An energetic group entity of the Ascended Masters, saints and their disciples; Divine Beings, Angels and Archangels; each grand soul of this group has lived an Earth life, bringing Light and paths of enlightenment to the Earth and Her people

Greatest disharmony: An apparent conflict, within which are the seeds for the greatest creation; a chaotic change that is breaking down old patterns, structures and beliefs, to make room for those of a higher consciousness

Guardianship: The help of the Ascended Masters and ngelic beings from higher dimensions, who seek to support us during our Earth lives; offered to all, though many humans neither accept nor understand this help

Hara line: A light vibrating Source and higher resonance of energy frequencies, passing through a person's energetic core

Heart-mind: The higher mind, led by the heart instead of logic; the place of deciphering truth from lies and misinformation

Heart-mind intelligence: The inner reality and consciousness of the sacred heart

Heightened sensitivity: Being intently aware of the Oneness; a perception that extends well beyond the five human senses

High vibrational energy: Light and energetic frequencies that resonate on a very pure and high level, relating to the Oneness of Divinity

Higher Self/Spirit Self: The higher aspect of anyone or anything; that which is part of God, the Holy Spirit

Holders of the Matrix of Light: Referring to those in greater Divine service; also known as Holders of the Divine Light; holders of Light frequencies that constantly charge the collective field while waiting for humanity's ascension

Holographic world or universe: The consciousness that creates the image of all that is around us; the mind-creation of the third-dimensional reality; also, the illusion of solid matter; the image and apparent realness of the universe around us, which is divided into levels of consciousness called dimensions

Holy Spirit: The Spirit Essence of Everything; Divine Feminine; Divine Mother; the Great Birther; the Godhead consciousness, the Is-ness that all are an individual component of; the Wholeness of Spirit; the totality of All, the One consciousness; the One; Mother God; Mother Mary, Quan Yin, Anu and Isis in our world, called Holy Spirit in the Grand World; the essence of Allness; the force and form of all existence; the vibration of Oneness, Wholeness, Light; the I Am

Holy temple: The awareness of inner consciousness, where the Holy Spirit resides

Humble Oneness: Freeing oneself from the lower ego and moving into the higher self; seeing that all are part of the One

I AM: The name of God; the phrase that activates Divine consciousness and enables living in higher consciousness; pure essence, undivided

I Am Presence: Realizing and having the greater memory that the Holy Spirit is within all

Illusion: The belief in the solidity or reality of matter; being deeply asleep during one's life on Earth; living in the dualistic delusion of separation and separate consciousness

Imbalance: Living without connection to one's center point; emphasizing the masculine over the feminine energies; being out of harmony; loss of inner Peace

Imprint: A vibration that leaves a stamp of awareness in a person's consciousness, memory, personality or place

Inalienable rights: Humanity's right to create joy in Earth lives; Divine rights that can never be fully taken away

Individual component: The unique energy signature of each created person or thing; part of the Holy Spirit or Source

Inner Center: The inner place of heart and spirit where the Christed Light is contained

Innocence: The essence of the nature of Divinity; seeing all as if seeing through the eyes of a small child

Junier, the Second Moon: A satellite body; its vibration was used to harness universal energies; it carried all Earth knowledge

Karma: Cause and effect; causal effect; the result of our actions and beliefs, which we must work out and resolve during our time on Earth

Karma's workshop: A metaphor referring to staying in fear and doubt, which leads one to attract the same environment again and again, until higher consciousness brings Peace

Kingdom of God: A holy place created within all; the holy inner temple

Kingdom of Heaven: Called the Grand World by those who inhabit it; a place of no separation; the higher reality

Knights Templar: An order of knights, founded in 1118 CE, to protect pilgrims traveling to the Holy Land; protectors of the wisdom, ancestry, lineage and knowledge of Jesus and the Holy Mother

Lemuria: A lost continent in the Pacific Ocean, which enjoyed a Golden Age of higher consciousness until its demise

Light or Light frequencies: The Love and enlightening higher energies of the Holy Spirit, Jesus, the Divine, the Christed consciousness and all within the Divine Matrix

Light Body: The crystalline structure of the New Human's physical body, of the fifth dimensions and higher; a body able to absorb the intensive Light frequencies increasingly being showered upon humankind and the Earth

Lightworkers: Agents of Divine Light; members of the soul groups who volunteered to come to Earth during Her ascension; those spreading the words and blessings of higher consciousness; those walking the Golden Path to enlightenment

Manifesting: Charging the fields of energy and photons with either positive or negative thought and emotion, to attract positive or negative people and situations; creation in a higher dimensional realm that is then brought into physical reality in the Earthly realm

Master: The knowledge of being a Christed One; one who actualizes that they are Holy Spirit in body

Master-verse: The Union of the Divine Mind and all of its units of consciousness; all that exists in matter and in spirit

Matrices of Light: Frequencies of higher Light, woven into crystalline structures in and around the Earth, to aid human enlightenment and ascension

Medulla: The brainstem, located at the back of the head, above the neck; an ancient holy memory point that can be accessed via meditation; also, a point of focus that can enable inter-dimensional travel

Messages of Truth: Jesus' and other Ascended Masters' messages, brought to those willing to hear and learn, at all times in human history

Mineral Kingdom: The rocks, soil and minerals of Earth, which when in unison with the Divine Mother, oscillate with the vibrations of Peace; part of the Earth's aliveness, with a spirit and a soul consciousness

Mission of Service: Realization of our higher identity and life purpose; awareness that all are pure Love and intelligence; service of spreading the message of Light, Love and Peace during one's Earth life

Mother Earth: The soul, spirit and person of Earth; Earth's vibration, which emits sustaining rays of Light to humanity, the physical planet, and the plant, animal and mineral kingdoms; a cosmic body that all can communicate with

Multi-dimensional reality: The many dimensions that exist simultaneously in the universes, or multiverse

Mystical Christ: The consciousness of being in center point and holding a higher awareness and heightened sense of peace and Oneness; actualizing the Divinity that is within us; Christ coming again to the Earth within human consciousness

Mystical Wisdom: Divine knowledge, perception and understanding; that which greatly exceeds the level of third-dimensional human understanding

Namaste: A Hindu greeting; meaning "I bow to you. The Divine in me salutes the Divine in you."

Nanosecond: One billionth of a second

New World: A grand change in consciousness; the awareness of the consciousness of the Divine Feminine birthing new evolution; the Earth's ascent into the fourth and fifth dimensions

No-Time: An awareness that the linear concept of time is a human creation; the eternal Now; awareness of the present moment as the only moment that exists

One consciousness: Conscious awareness that all within the universe are intrinsically part of the Oneness that is the Holy Spirit

Oneness: A state of Love and higher awareness; a blending of inner consciousness and outer living; having Christed awareness or Christed consciousness

Oneness Awareness: A consciousness of the Unity of Holy Spirit, the I Am; the awareness that all in existence is one in the universe

Open channel: One who receives wisdom and communication from the higher realms

Open Light of the Christ: A pure being, radiating the miracles of Light and higher energies in their individual qualities of life, and in the collective field of Earth

Oscillation: A continual, uninterrupted radiating outward of a vibratory, energetic wave

Peace: The higher path to Love and God; blending with Holy Spirit; a vibration of calm that becomes fully activated within one as one attains the awareness of being the Holy Spirit; center point consciousness; the power that creates harmony and Love and assists the collective conscious, by creating waves of vibration that penetrate through the collective field

Peaceful Lights: Healing, radiant light bodies

Piercing the veil of consciousness: Expanding beyond the lower ego; seeing through the veil that separates the dimensions of consciousness; moving into the fifth dimension and becoming aware of multi-dimensional realities

Pineal gland activation: An active awareness of the Christed self; receiving the higher frequencies of energy and Light that transmit higher knowing, and the intuitive wisdom and insight of the higher realms; also, activation of the gifts of telepathy and foresight

Project Peace: A momentum of Peace that Mother Mary has brought forward upon the Earth

Purity of Wisdom: Ultimate truth and integrity; alignment with the Oneness of all; alignment with the Holy Spirit

Radiating Peace: A state achieved, as Holy Spirit suggests, by placing the left hand on the heart, and extending the right hand outwards; an act of radiating Love out to others; also, radiating that frequency into crystals

Rays of Light energy: Divine energies helping to activate our DNA/RNA and chakras; energies that enable the opening of the heart, heart/mind and higher mind connections to Holy Spirit

Reactive behavior: Reacting to another in anger, from the lower ego

Rebirthing: To regain higher awareness; to re-awaken to the Holy Spirit, knowing that the Holy Spirit was simply asleep in us; to begin a new life in higher consciousness

Reborn: A rebirth, with the knowing and understanding of the Holy Spirit within

Receptive: Open, with a silent mind; allowing oneself to feel, allow, and to be more open to the new changes; a state that requires faith

Refined vibration: Blending of humanness into the Divine Self

Regenerated Source: The Holy Spirit, reborn into human beings

Rejoicing realm: A reference made by Jesus, describing the creative passion and power of the Divine on Earth

Releasing karmic patterns: Understanding Love and Oneness; releasing all belief in separation; releasing the yin/yang patterns of happiness/sadness, joy/suffering, stability/chaos, thus freeing oneself

Sacred breath: Breathing with the intention to come into center point; breathing with an intent to enter a higher state of consciousness

Sacred Fire: Life force; sacred consciousness; accessed by connecting with one's Divine Self

Sacred Heart: The Christed heart within; the sacred intention of one's consciousness; sharing the joy of Spirit, the blessings of Love and purity of Oneness; the Holy Mother's compassionate love

Sacred Mind: A state of consciousness held with the intention to hold the light and truth within

Sacred Truth: The Light and wisdom of non-judgment and Unconditional Love

Separation: A creation of third-dimensional reality; a loss of understanding the grander aspect of the Divine Feminine and the Divine Masculine; a state of mind separate from Love; seeing another person as not part of oneself; excessive masculine energy

Shimmering consciousness: The beauty of pure Peace and harmony; the expression of pure Love

Soul: The guiding force of the human being; part of one's essence, sacred self and higher aspect

Soul contracts: Agreements with other souls, made and entered into before every incarnation, which can be renegotiated

Soul negotiation: Intervention, such as by an energy healer, spirit guide or loved one, who requests that the soul of someone find a resolution that fulfills the path of learning in a less painful way

Soul mission: The objective of the higher self, in connection to the Holy Spirit and Oneness; path of soul growth and contribution

Source: The Holy Spirit, the Great Divine Mother and Father; the Oneness; the All-That-Is; the Universal Mind; Divine Energy

Source consciousness: The mind of the "I Am" within human beings and within all existence; the awareness of being One with Source, as well as an individual expression of Source

Source DNA and RNA: The codes of perfection carried within Source; different from the biological DNA and RNA

Spirit in matter: Existing in this third-dimensional reality with awareness that all is from and of Divine Source Energy

Spreading the Light: Spending one's Earth life healing, teaching, spreading the word of Source; sharing wisdom on Earthly life lessons

Sunrise: The time of day for blending with the Ascended Masters, allowing ourselves a conscious exchange and acknowledging the Masters

Temple of the Ascended Masters: State of consciousness accessed by going within to one's heart and higher self/higher mind; creating an inner vision of a meeting place of the Masters

Thirteenth dimension: The realm of the Holy Spirit; the dimension of Oneness

Thousand years of Peace: Originally referred to in scripture as the thousand years of Peace anchored into Earth, after which Peace will reign on this planet forever

Time: Largely a creation of the third dimension, as in the Grand World of Heaven; there is no time but the present moment

Transformation: Allowing and creating a shift to higher awareness, higher consciousness

Transition: Utilizing a higher frequency to birth new matter or new consciousness

Transmutation: Humankind's energy of destruction, necessary in order to tranform itself into readiness to enter into the new higher vibration of the New World

Unconditional Love: Constant, kind, forgiving and unending acceptance of all by the Divine; accessed by coming out of the lower ego; the most sacred vibration in the universe

Veils of consciousness: The density of energy and lack of spiritual insight that blocks human consciousness from awareness of the dimensions and varying levels of consciousness; exist only in this holographic universe, as illusions of separation, now thinning as humanity awakens

Virgin: In the higher realms, the Divine Feminine who, without a male, births all that is, by seeding, conception, and birthing; the Great Birther; differing from the meaning in the realm of matter, which is one who has not had sexual intercourse

Vulnerability: State of being passive and receptive, as Mary, the Holy Spirit exemplifies, requiring quieting and stilling the mind and increasing inner alignment with Peacefulness and Love

Wave of Peace: A calming, all-loving vibration that emerges from within, sent out to the collective or individual consciousness

Wisdom: The Holy Spirit, known as the Grand Wisdom of existence

Notes

Chapter Four

1 James Rado & Gerome Ragni (lyrics), and Galt MacDermot (music), "Aquarius/Let the Sunshine In," in *Hair*, (recorded by The 5th Dimension, 1967), Broadway musical, *Metro Lyrics*, accessed July 10, 2013, http://www.metrolyrics.com/aquarius-lyrics-hair.html.

Chapter Thirteen

1 "Titles of Our Lady from the Litany of Loreto," *Salve Maria Regina*, accessed August 5, 2013, http://www.salvemariaregina.info/SalveMariaRegina/SMR-169/Star.htm.

2 Pius XII, "Ad Caeli Reginam: Encyclical of Pope Pius XII on Proclaiming the Queenship of Mary to the Venerable Brethren, the Patriarchs, Primates, Archbishops, Bishops, and Other Local Ordinaries in Peace and Communion with the Holy See," (given at Rome, from St. Peter's, October 11, 1954), the Vatican, accessed August 20, 2013, http://www.vatican.va/holy_father/pius_xii/encyclicals/documents/hf_p-xii_enc_11101954_ad-caelireginam_en.html.

3 "Consecration to or Through Our Lady?" *Eternal World Television Network (EWTN)*, accessed on August 20, 2013, http://www.ewtn.com/library/MARY/MARCON.HTM.

4 "Titles of Our Lady from the Litany of Loreto."

5 Pius XII, "Ad Caeli Reginam."

6 Pius XII, "Ad Caeli Reginam."

7 John Paul II, Homily given at The Basilica of Our Lady of Guadalupe, Mexico City, "Apostolic Journey to America," January 23, 1999, *Libreria Editrice Vaticana*, accessed August 6, 2013, http://www.vatican.va/holy_father/john_paul_ii/homilies/1999/documents/hf_jp-ii_hom_19990123_mexico-guadalupe_en.html.

8 "Mary, Queen of Heaven, Watches Over Her Children, Pope Says at Audience," *Catholic News Service*, August 22, 2012, accessed August 6, 2013, http://www.catholicnews.com/data/stories/cns/1203534 htm.

9 Pius XII, "Ad Caeli Reginam," excerpts from sections 1-40.

10 John Paul II, "Apostolic Journey to America."

11 John Paul II, Encyclical Letter Dominum et Vivificantem, "The Holy Spirit in the Life of the Church and the World," *EWTN Online Services*, May 5, 1986, accessed August 6, 2013, http://www.ewtn.com/library/encyc/jp2giver.htm.

12 John Paul II, "The Holy Spirit in the Life of the Church and the World."

13 John Paul II, "The Holy Spirit in the Life of the Church and the World."

14 John A. Tvedtnes, "Mary and the Tree of Life," *Book of Mormon Research*, accessed August 6, 2013, http://bookofmormonresearch.org/book_of_mormon_articles/mary-and-the-tree-of-life.

15 Carl E. Braaten and Robert W. Jenson, *Mary, Mother of God*, (Grand Rapids, Mich.: Eerdmans Publishing Co., 2004), 84.

16 Francis, "The Holy Spirit Renews Our Lives," *Vatican Radio*, July 6, 2013, accessed August 6, 2013, http://www.news.va/en/news/pope-francis-the-holy-spirit-renews-our-lives.

17 "Titles of Our Lady from the Litany of Loreto."

18 "Titles of Our Lady from the Litany of Loreto."

19 "Titles of Our Lady from the Litany of Loreto."

20 "Titles of Our Lady from the Litany of Loreto."

21 "Titles of Our Lady from the Litany of Loreto."

22 Tvedtnes, "Mary and the Tree of Life."

23 Pius XII, "Ad Caeli Reginam."

24 "Titles of Our Lady from the Litany of Loreto."

25 "Titles of Our Lady from the Litany of Loreto."

26 "Venus Transit: A Trinity of Energy; the Divine Union of the Sun, Venus, Gaia and All Upon Her," *Golden Age of Gaia*, June 5, 2012, accessed August 16, 2013 http:/goldenageofgaia.com/2012/06/venus-transit-a-trinity-of-energy-the-divine-union-of-the-sun-venus-gaia-and-all-upon-her/.

27 "Venus Transit."

28 Shekina Rose, "Venus Transit: Anchoring the Rose Ray Codes & Ascension Symptoms Planetary Alert," *Spirit Library*, June 4, 2012, http://spiritlibrary.com/shekina-rose-blue-ray/venus-transit-anchoring-the-rose-ray-codes-ascension-symptoms-planetary-alert.

29 Shekina Rose, "Venus Transit."

30 Shekina Rose, "Blue Ray Awakening," *Constant Contact*, 2010, accessed August 16, 2013 http://archive.constantcontact.com/fs014/1101389983006/archive/1109301867419.html.

Chapter Fourteen

1 Annice Booth and Elizabeth Clare Prophet, *Mary Magdalene and the Divine Feminine: Jesus' Lost Teachings on Woman*, (Gardner, Montana: Summit University Press, 2005), Kindle locations 360-361.

2 Elaine Pagels, *The Gnostic Gospels*, (New York: Vintage Books, 1989) 60–61, in Booth and Prophet, Kindle locations 603-605.

3 Pagels, *The Gnostic Gospels*, 57, in Booth and Prophet, Kindle locations 1814-1815.

4 Rosemary Radford Ruether, *Womanguides* (Boston: Beacon Press, 1985) 24, in Lil Abdo Osborn, "Female Representations of the Holy Spirit in Bahá'í and Christian writings and their implications for gender roles," *Bahá'í Studies Review*, 4:1, London: Association for Baha'i Studies English-Speaking Europe, 1994, accessed August 16, 2013, http://bahai-library.com/abdo_female_holy-spirit.

5 Booth and Prophet, Kindle locations 722-725.

6 Tertullian, *On the Apparel of Women*, Book 1, Chapter 1, in *New Advent*, accessed August 20, 2013 http://www.newadvent.org/fathers/0402.htm.

7 Dirk Gillabel, "Gnosticism: Answers to Who We Are," *Soul Guidance*, 2001, accessed August 17, 2013, http://www.soul-guidance.com/houseofthesun/gnosticism.htm.

8 Gillabel, "Gnosticism."

9 Elaine Pagels, Interview with Robert Siegel on National Public Radio, "Ancient Paper Suggests Jesus May Have Been Married," radio show, accessed August 17, 2013, *http://www.npr.org/2012/09/19/161436258/ancient-paper-suggests-jesus-may-have-been-married.*

10 Pagels, NPR interview.

11 "There's No Conspiracy to Silence the Gnostics," *Theoblogy*, accessed August 16, 2013, http://www.patheos.com/blogs/tonyjones/2012/09/21/theres-no-conspiracy-to-silence-the-gnostics-questions-that-haunt/.

12 David Frawley, *Wisdom of the Ancient Seers: Mantras of the Rig Veda* (Salt Lake City, Utah: Passage Press, 1992), 54, in Booth and Prophet, Kindle location 1116.

13 Booth and Prophet, Kindle locations 1097-1100.

14 Booth and Prophet, Kindle locations 1188-1192.

15 Booth and Prophet, Kindle locations 1128-1130.

16 James M. Robinson, "Very Goddess and Very Man: Jesus' Better Self," in Karen L. King, ed., *Images of the Feminine in Gnosticism* (Harrisburg, Pa.: Trinity Press International, 2000), 117, in Booth and Prophet, Kindle locations 1196-1201.

17 Acts of Thomas 5:50, in R.P. Nettlehorst, "More Than Just a Controversy: All About the Holy Spirit," *Journal of Quartz Hill School of Theology*, accessed August 15, 2013, http://www.theology.edu/journal/volume3/spirit.htm.

18 Robinson, in Booth and Prophet, Kindle locations 1200-1201.

19 The Gospel of Philip 60.1, in Robinson, 146, in Booth and Prophet, Kindle Locations 1208-1209.

20 Booth and Prophet, Kindle locations 1230-1234.

21 Booth and Prophet, Kindle locations 1224-1226.

22 Gershom G. Scholem, *Major Trends in Jewish Mysticism* (New York Schocken Books, 1961), 230, in Booth and Prophet, Kindle locations 1230-1234.

23 Caitlín Matthews, *Sophia: Goddess of Wisdom*, The Aquarian Press, 1992, 179-90, accessed August 14, 2013, http://adishakti.org/_/goddess_remains_the_esoteric_heartbeat_of_islam.htm.

24 Laurence Galian, "The Centrality of the Divine Feminine in Sufism," (paper presented at the Second Annual Hawaii International Conference on Arts & Humanities," Honolulu, 2004), accessed August 14, 2013, http://www.adishakti.org/_/centrality_of_the_divine_feminine_in_sufism.htm#sthash.n9UZhio8.dpuf.

25 Jalāl ad-Dīn Muhammad Rūmī, quoted by Galian, "The Centrality of the Divine Feminine in Sufism."

26 Galian, "The Centrality of the Divine Feminine in Sufism."

27 Rick Hoyt, sermon on "The Divine Mother," 2006, accessed August 15, 2013, http://www.adishakti.org/_/divine_mother_ricky_hoyt.htm#sthash.C2UhUKsY.dpuf.

28 Hoyt, "The Divine Mother."

Upcoming Book by

Kevin Peter Kelly and Marina Nikole Kelly

Find excerpts of these books and their scheduled release dates at www.DedicatedLightworker.com:

Jesus, the Prince of Peace

The Book of Masters

Lessons of Enlightenment

Be in Peace

Jesus, the Greatest Healer

The Sacred Life of Joseph

Quan Yin, Goddess of Compassion and Mercy

The New Human Template

Be in Peace

Notes